MW00616192

The Raw,
Rowdy World
of Poker

Also by the Author:

THE GREAT AMERICAN PASTIME

THE RAW, ROWDY WORLD OF POKER

Allen Dowling

SOUTH BRUNSWICK AND NEW YORK:
A. S. BARNES AND COMPANY

LONDON: THOMAS YOSELOFF LTD

© 1973 by A. S. Barnes and Co., Inc.

A. S. Barnes and Co., Inc.
Cranbury, New Jersey 08512

Thomas Yoseloff Ltd
108 New Bond Street
London W1Y OQX, England

Library of Congress Cataloging in Publication Data

Dowling, Allen Nicholas, 1900–
  The raw, rowdy world of poker.

  1. Poker—Anecdotes, facetiae, satire, etc.
I. Title
GV1253.D617   795.4'12'0207   74–39353
ISBN 0–498–01167–4

Printed in the United States of America

Contents

Introduction

In a large sense poker is simply an arena for humans in which to cavort with their emotions more or less showing. Whether you are a good player or only mediocre, you expose at least in some degree your personality traits, principles, philosophy of life if you have gone to the trouble of formulating one, and sometimes even your innermost thoughts, in the process of reacting to the various situations and crises as they arise, and as good fortune and bad take turns smiling on you or bouncing you around.

It is not the same as when you ignore your inhibitions under alcoholic influence and let your true personality ooze out, although this can happen in poker, too, and may on occasion be disassociated from the game itself. The manner in which the curtain is pulled aside in poker, sans Scotch or bourbon or other stimulant, is altogether different. It is almost always a piecemeal exposition, a succession of little things that may seem to have no significance, but eventually the unveiling is complete, at least in most cases. I am constrained to add that it would be most unusual to get an accurate line on an individual with whom you are playing for the first time. Mystery writers and others have had murderers and other criminals give themselves away to the slick detective under the pressure of some exciting betting situation, and you can buy it if you wish—but take a big discount.

If you play poker with somebody long enough to believe you have him tabbed exactly as he is, you could be right. However, it usually is not the individuals as much as it is the *types* of humans you learn to fathom.

The difference between good poker playing and bad is not necessarily determined by educational advantages. An illiterate, savvy to the subtleties of human behavior, might have a better chance than a Rhodes scholar. Incidentally, the average poker game is not by any stretch of the imagination a struggle of razor-sharp wits. In most games there is usually one or perhaps two good or fair players, and the others are run-of-the-mill.

There is little doubt that, because poker is just people, it does not produce any more outstanding players than life does sensational successes. The reason is pretty obvious. The average individual figures that the Hall of Fame is already overcrowded, so he only puts himself to the strain of getting by. The average poker player is happy if he can stay in the game.

In spite of the fact that they are nearly always short on authenticity, movie and television directors frequently capitalize on the dramatic quality of the poker sequence. This is just about impossible with other card games because the human factor is subordinate. How fascinated do you think an audience would be if the hero were sweating it out for a fortune with the heroine's honor as a side bet, and victory depended upon successfully finessing through the leering heavy? Even the bridge experts probably would stifle a yawn.

If you play a lot of poker you eventually will come up with some pretty solid convictions. My number one is that people are funny all right—but usually when they are not trying.

There is a fable about the three blind men who examined an elephant by touch and later reported their findings. They presented three different ideas of what an elephant looks like—with no version even coming close to reality. People who know about poker only from casual play or from what they see in plays, read, or hear may not be any better informed. I wrote the sketches and stories that comprise this book because I wanted to resolve some of the existing confusion—even at the risk of starting a new series of bum arguments.

Allen Dowling

The Raw,
Rowdy World
of Poker

1
The Policy Game

At least one absorbing (and important) aspect of no-limit stud poker often occurs *after* all the chips of the pot participants have been wagered, provided it is possible for the player with the best hand to take "insurance."

The foregoing is not intended to mystify or confound. In some games of the type mentioned the players form themselves into a "mutual" company, sharing risks and profits. In the private game, in which I have done considerable playing, there is an arbitrary factor of 28 as the hub of the operation, the odds against the best hand being outdrawn ranging from 28-to-one up to, theoretically, 28-to-28, or 28-to-29, or 28-to even a higher figure. In the latter instance the player with the best hand would be laying odds, due to the fact that more than 28 cards possibly could improve his opponent's hand. The following are examples of how insurance works.

At the start of a pot a player with ace high is challenged by a player with a queen, and before another card is dealt all the chips of both players are in the center of the table. The hands are then exposed and prove that it is two aces against two queens. The player with the aces, if he wants insurance, can get 28-to-two that the next card will not be a queen to his opponent because there are only two queens remaining in the deck. (The discard is not taken into consideration, only the cards that come out *after* insurance prevails, figuring in the computation of the odds.) If neither

13

hand helps, the odds then go to 28-to-five, because the holder of the queens not only may draw one of the queens, but also one of the three cards that match the one he has drawn. If the next cards to fall change nothing, the odds before the final card are now 28-to-eight, there now being one of three additional cards that the hand with the queens may draw.

The amount of insurance that the holder of the best hand takes usually is governed by the size of the pot and how much of a gamble the holder wishes to take. If he is on the conservative side he may want to take enough to guarantee a fair profit in case his hand is outdrawn. This is known as insuring the pot; if otherwise, he may desire only to insure the amount of his own investment. Such factors as the nearness to the end of the game, or whether the insuree is a winner or a loser also determine the extent of his coverage. (Insurance over pot value is barred.)

In a different type of situation with, say, only one card to fall, and at which point all the chips of the pot participants are wagered, the player with the best hand may have two sixes, and his opponent a straight open on both ends, king high. There are eight cards (always theoretically) that will make the straight, and 12 cards that will pair one of the four cards comprising the possible straight. So the rate in this case is 28-to-20.

When insurance prevails, the insured may change before the completion of the deal. Going back to the original example, the player with the two queens may make two pairs before the last card falls, and if the player with the aces has not helped, may himself take insurance. When a situation of this kind occurs the mutual company is in bad shape, because one way or another there will be a payoff.

If a player with the best hand wants to see what he will draw on any turn, provided he is dealt to first, and if he does not help, *then* wants to insure his hand, the price doubles. If the odds had been 28-to-three they would jump to 28-to-six, and so on.

At the end of the game if there is an insurance profit, it is divided equally among the players, and if there is a loss, it is prorated equally.

It probably is obvious that the mutual company has all the best

14

of it, but there is nothing wrong with that because all the players are on a par as company members. One of the quirks favorable to the company is that the insurance is on each turn, not at a flat price that the best hand will or will not stand up, and so as many as three separate investments may be required. Another, and very desirable, circumstance is that the best hand also can help, usually having as good a potential, theoretically, as the inferior hand.

There is also another situation which can, and sometimes *does,* occur. For example, with two cards to fall, the best hand is outdrawn on the first of these, the cost of the holder's insurance investment being $25. His opponent, who has helped, then takes insurance (or perhaps does not) and the original best hand helps on the last card and wins the pot. In spite of the fact that the holder of the original best hand actually earned a payoff when outdrawn, he not only does not get it, but, as he has won the pot, his $25 is put into the insurance pool. So, in effect, in a situation of that kind, the player can lose, but cannot win. Slightly outrageous? Not really, because *all* the players are potentially victims and beneficiaries.

As stated at the outset, watching the progress of an insurance pot is fascinating to everybody because the outcome will represent profit or loss. In a recent game, when the pot was worth about $400, one player had an ace in the hole, king, queen in sight, and the other player, with the best hand, had an ace in the hole, ace, eight in sight. So it was two aces against one ace, the rate in favor of the best hand being 28-to-one on the next turn. The dealer accidentally dealt too quickly, or so it seemed, depriving the player with the two aces of an opportunity to insure, and the player with the ace, king, queen caught the fourth ace. His opponent drew a nine, so now the insurance situation was reversed, and the player with the first two aces could have won with six cards, three eights and three nines. The player who drew the case ace invested $42 in insurance, and his hand stood up. The loser moaned that he had intended to take 28-to-one ten times, and he probably had, but the insurance company saved $280 by the lucky mishap.

An old-timer in the game, intrigued by the incident just recounted, unburdened himself as follows: "You know," he said, "it's a sweet thing indeed to be able to get 28-to-one that a case card will or will not be drawn, and odds in other situations in keeping with what is considered to be arithmetically sound. Yet," he concluded, "if you simply take the position that the desired card either will or won't fall, that it's either there or it isn't, why should the price be better than even money?"

2
Call the Wagon

The most accomplished Hollywood director might pick up an idea or two if he watched a mitt-joint performance now and then. The setting usually is a tavern or second-rate nightclub. The trap is a no-limit poker game off to one side.

Enter the principal—the pigeon. He may just blunder in or he may have been steered. If he resists routine overtures, one of the players asks the pigeon to play a couple of hands for him while he makes a telephone call and adds that they will split any profit. The pigeon wins—a little. Then comes the hand. The pigeon has aces back-to-back. His opponent has a king in sight, and they start betting. With one card to come the pigeon has ace, queen, and a small card in sight. His opponent has a king and two small cards in sight. The pigeon is told that if he likes his hand he may bet all he wants, even go into his pocket if he wishes. The pigeon catches another small card and his opponent grabs an ace. There is more betting if the pigeon is not clean, and the hands are then turned over. The pigeon loses because his opponent has an ace in the hole and two aces, king high, beat two aces, queen high.

The word *mitt* is a common term for *hand*. The idea is that you are dealt a set-up hand or mitt in a certain establishment. Many poker players refer to any kind of business where they figure that customers get the worst of it as a *mitt joint*.

Mitt joints are responsible for the bad name public poker clubs sometimes get because the uninitiated do not bother to make fine distinctions. The fact of the matter is that a mitt joint is nothing but a deadfall, a bunco routine with poker as the bait. All the players are part of the setup. The only revenue is from cheating suckers.

Poker has two- and three-quarters strikes on it as far as the bluenoses are concerned because it is just about the only card game there is—excepting banking games such as blackjack and faro—that holds little or no interest without wagering. Bridge and gin rummy frequently are played for high stakes but they are also played for kicks, as are any number of other card games and other recreational games, such as chess and checkers. Putting your skill and experience on the line often provides sufficient challenge to sustain interest. This does not work in poker because mechanically the game is absurdly simple. It is only when the gain motive exists that you have any inclination to get your best grip.

Unless there is a tough puritanical ordinance to the contrary, you may play poker in nearly all communities without fear of being arrested, provided the game is on a noncommercial basis. This simply means that only the winners may profit. If there is a cut or rakeoff, it is a House game and becomes, in most localities, a gambling operation and accordingly falls afoul of the law.

People who like to play poker but lack the opportunity insofar as games at somebody's house or a private club are concerned often permit themselves to become quite annoyed at what they consider to be unjust discrimination. It costs to operate a poker game, the big items being overhead and personnel, so unless the game provides an income its operation obviously is out of the

17

question. This situation narrows the possibilities for players who do not run with a poker-playing set or who cannot afford club membership.

If local laws against poker playing are being enforced (except under certain conditions already noted), the public-club and tavern games (where it is to the interest of the operators to protect the players) get the same attention as mitt joints. Frequently the loud squawk of a mitt-joint victim will touch off a drive against all poker games. This gives city editors a chance to get hot-seat poker headlines on page one, which is no knock to street sales.

3
Left-handed Apology

I have in other works blasted the movies and television for distorting the image of poker and, in many instances, grossly misinforming the public. They would have you believe that Hoyle is a poker authority, that acquiring skill in poker is a matter of attaining proficiency by assiduous practice, like a marksman preparing for a turkey shoot, and they would have you believe that among all poker players there is a champion, an Olympian personage whose talents at the round table cannot be matched. Further, they would have you believe . . . but why go on? It is seldom indeed that the poker sequence is buttressed by what could be considered authenticity, even though realism usually would strengthen rather than weaken the situation. Probably the greatest goof the movies ever committed (which I have presented in detail elsewhere) was in having a dazzlingly clever mitt (crooked) dealer win an immense pot by bluffing under circumstances and conditions shockingly absurd even to the average second-rate poker player.

One of the most amusing movie and television routines in poker games, especially when the stakes are enormous, is for a player, whose turn it is to act, to say, after a bet has been made, "I call . . ." and follow this declaration of his intent by placing the requisite amount in the pot. Having done this he then hesitatingly adds as a dreamy afterthought, ". . . and raise," and proceeds to do just that with chips or money or both, his physiognomy complacent and assured. The writers of such tableaux probably do not know themselves that a grave poker error has been committed, or, if they do know, which is improbable, they are counting on the ignorance of nearly all of the viewers, who most likely are not acquainted with the finer points of poker jurisprudence.

The explanation of the above is simply this: the player who *called* and then *raised* made *two* bets, in poker language a *string* bet, which is strictly prohibited in any company where the basic rules of the game are observed. This unquestionably is the custom in serious poker games, especially stud, wherein the violation could have important consequences that could easily affect the size and outcome of the pot. So strict is the rule that even if a player whose turn it is to act says nothing, but after making the call tries to go back to his stack for the purpose of raising, he would not be allowed to do so. If, prior to acting, he announces a raise and specifies the amount, he could then put the chips in the pot one at a time, if he chooses. The point is, only *one* bet can be made. To explain a bit further, so that there can be no misunderstanding, in some games (I really believe, in most) shoving chips into the pot in excess of the previous bet, without going back to the stack but minus a spoken declaration, is a legal raise.

The real purpose of this dissertation is, as the title implies, to bestow an accolade on the movies and television for at least one important attitude that gives credence and approval to another position of mine (in which I find myself at variance with most of the poker experts, self-styled or otherwise). They advocate the playing of offshoot or variant forms of poker such as seven-card stud, baseball, high-low, etc. There has never been, to my knowledge, a poker sequence in the movies or television that was not based on the standard five-card game. This fact is of itself significant because it is what has to be considered objective evidence of the fascination and dramatic quality of unadorned poker, as it came down to us from the game's stalwart progenitors, including some of this country's most famous personages.

Not too long ago I saw a most interesting television documentary on the subject of authentic photographs from the early days in the Old West that were by pioneer photographers, who incurred incredible risks and hardships for the sake of their art. Portrayed were wagon trains, galloping Indians, buffalo hunts, frontier towns, army posts garrisoned by colorful cavalry units, and scenes of great plains and wild, mountainous terrain. What impressed me most, in spite of my admiration for the heroes of the lens and tripod, was a statement made by the narrator. He said, bluntly, that when attacking Indians outnumbered their opponents, there was no such thing as the Indians losing, depictions in the movies being to the contrary. This may or may not be true, but as a devotee of historical truths I was shaken a bit, yet I have to believe that if generally so there surely were exceptions. However, if the movie makers have not hesitated at distortions and lapses in westerns, it is easily understandable that poker would not be spared, but I am happy to report that they have mitigated the offense, by recognizing the validity of the standard game.

4
Leave 'Em Scowling

Some time back, when I was a regular player in a weekly table-stakes stud game, I was cursed with an uncomfortably long losing streak. Now, snapping out of a losing streak in an easy game usually means relatively speedy recovery, but in this situation such was not the case. The game was not soft by any means, because the players were mature, experienced, and conservative (the last by nature) in poker and all their other activities. Furthermore, they nearly all were the gabby, upper middle-class type, interested in the contemporary scene, especially politics and finance. This, as may have been expected, often slowed the action with too much discussion and chatter instead of serious poker. As a comparative newcomer to the group (and not en rapport with them in certain areas other than poker) I found the atmosphere too tranquil and unruffled, not at all conducive to poker feuds and antagonisms. Occasionally, though, there would be an exchange of banter, usually a couple calling each other tight, and both being absolutely right.

What I have just outlined was only a part of the problem. Overall, their attitude toward me was friendly (that is, in a poker sense), which was bad enough, but there was more. I was well aware that I was tabbed as a four-star tightwad, which often prevented my getting action with the best hand, but it was not all one-sided, because it made stealing small pots no trouble when my hand in sight *looked* strong, and I *played* it that way. Also, I could work an angle play with more chance of success than an adventurous player would have, such as paying a relatively substantial amount to pair an unsuspected hole card. However, both of these advantages existed to any real extent only when luck was not too bad, and even then did not go far enough. I simply had to get more action.

I knew from experience that there was one sure way to improve matters, simply by antagonizing the other players, to make them want to beat me, to create an image of myself as a disagreeable individual from whom winning would be an exquisite pleasure. But what could I do? I just could not come out and insult people. My odious character, as planned, had to be only as a poker player. So I laid low until the break for which I awaited arrived.

The game, as I have stated, was stud (standard, five-card poker, nothing wild), but if eight or fewer players were at the table, which sometimes was true for the entire evening, the dealer could deal draw, jacks or better to open. On an occasion when draw was allowed I dealt it every time it was my deal, but for a couple of hours not only did I not win a draw pot, I did not even have a good enough hand to play. Finally, I was able to open the pot, and when a couple of players passed, the player whose turn it was to act said to the remaining players (whose hands probably were weak since they had not opened when they had the opportunity), "Oh, let him win the ante, he hasn't won a draw pot tonight!"

At last I had my chance. I pretended to interpret the player's suggestion as being a gesture of sympathy toward a loser, and I so proclaimed in a deeply offended vein that sympathy was the one thing I did not crave. Then I added, as dramatically as I could without sounding too silly, that I would regard any player who made the slightest gesture of sympathy toward me as a bitter poker enemy, and would be at great pains to be lying in wait for him, especially if an opportunity existed for checking a cinch. I expanded the last to assert, vehemently, that as far as checking a cinch was concerned, it would be my greatest pleasure to do it to anybody.

The result was what I had expected. It dissolved any possibility of friendliness in the poker game (and perhaps out of it, too), but I felt that I had to give myself this edge. If I have indirectly implied that other players played sympathy with each other let me hasten to state that this generally was not the case, although it occasionally was in evidence. At any rate, my purpose was accomplished. I wanted every player to go after me at every opportunity, to get personal satisfaction as well as my chips when he racked me up.

5
Kentucky Derby Special

I played poker regularly some years back with a retired tugboat captain whose proudest possession was a gold medal presented to him for his skill at the game. It was a gift from his former waterfront cronies and was inscribed with a glowing testimonial to the many times he pinned their ears back. The captain wore it as a charm on his old-fashioned watch chain. He claimed that the token was inspired by the high sentimental regard in which he was held. It was more likely, however, that the players who chipped in for the medal figured that it was a pretty cheap price to pay to be rid of such a tough old tightwad.

It is not too often that poker players get medals or scrolls or other recognition of their talent. What they mainly get if they win too consistently is a lot of abuse, except in certain situations where the sordid gain motive actually is subordinate to the desire to triumph for the sheer glory of it.

I am personally innocent of any connection with poker games that reward other than materially. I have heard of such games, though, and recently interviewed a charter member of a select group whose weekly game is unique. One of the many unusual features of this game is the fact that a champion is declared at the end of each year, as is done in professional baseball and football leagues. He receives a handsome plaque, appropriately engraved.

They play rough and for keeps, even if they do think that copping the "Oscar" is big stuff. They play five-card, nothing-wild, no-limit stud, table stakes. They are all substantial citizens, financially speaking, the roster including professional men, industrialists, and merchants. The active coterie is limited to ten players and has never been known to be short-handed, because there is a horde of eager substitutes. When a permanent vacancy occurs among the regular players, the number one player on the substitute list gets first opportunity to join, but the vote of the remaining nine must be unanimous.

The locale of the game is a well-appointed room used solely for that purpose in the palatial home of one of the players. Play commences immediately after dinner and ends punctually at midnight. If you are hooked when the automatic time device sounds a buzzer, you are a dead duck until the following week.

This is one of the few poker games of which I know that operates an "insurance company." Details of the operation of this and other games that include insurance coverage (if all the chips of the pot participants have been wagered) are presented in another portion of this work. While it is not uncommon to take insurance against the best hand being outdrawn (this practice especially flourished during the heyday of the public clubs), this particular game probably gets credit for originating the method that is employed. In the public-club games you usually could get three-to-one or better that your hand, if best, would win, no matter how many cards were still to come, but in this game the insurance is limited to each remaining turn, if there is more than one card still to be dealt.

The game insurance company is no different from other insurance companies. It makes nothing but money. The profits not only pay all the ordinary expenses of the game, but there is enough for a big Kentucky Derby party each year. The players charter a private railroad car, stock up with whatever is needed in the way of fancy food and drink, and, with a couple of crack Pullman porters at their beck and call, play poker coming and going on the twenty-six hour run between Louisville and their home town. They not only have their own custom-made poker table—a collapsible affair that sets sturdily when anchored into position—but they also bring their own shaded drop-light that is suspended dead center over the table. It also is custom-made and anchors so firmly that no amount of swaying disturbs it.

You can only turn green with envy when you hear of such doings, and perhaps drool at the prospect of easy pickings if you were favored with an opportunity to substitute occasionally. Yet there could be difficulties. Players with big bankrolls can be rough customers in high-stake games, and there also is the bad angle of the time limit. Further, the player who gave me the dope came up promptly with too many right answers to a few "innocent" questions I asked about some little-known features of topflight poker. The chances are pretty good that if they did invite me, I would "pass."

6
"There are stranger things . . ."

I once had a job that brought me into contact with underprivileged families. I frequently had to make decisions that were just routine work to me but that could be pretty important to them. As a precaution against possible injustice it sometimes was necessary to steam myself up to believe stories that sounded like nothing but fiction, but which occasionally proved to be true. My subordinates had me pegged for a gullible sap but this did not bother me. I simply adopted the policy of giving the benefit of any doubt to people. If it later developed that they had pulled my leg, it would be time enough to lower the boom.

It was this schooling in not arbitrarily rejecting what seemed to be eyewash that prompted me to run down the story of the strangest poker game of them all. I eventually located an old bum in a Poydras street trap of New Orleans's skid row who had heard it a dozen times from the horse's mouth, a wino pal who had been one of the players but who later had perished during World War II when the tanker on which he was a watchman was torpedoed. Two others of the five who had played also were dead, and a fourth was reportedly still fuzzy-minded in the state booby hatch, to which he had been hauled a couple of days after the game.

The sawbuck I showed the derelict, which he no doubt translated mentally into so many pints of muscatel and sherry, made him positively garrulous. Here is what he told me, minus about a hundred unimportant details.

Some twenty years or so previously in this same neighborhood a smart operator named Angelo ran a stud game in the back room of his bookie joint. The principal pigeon was a prosperous butcher, a fat squarehead known only as the Dutchman. One night the Dutchman came in early, before Angelo showed up, so the other players started the game for him. The longer they played the more the Dutchman won. In fact, he could not lose. Everything he did was right. Pretty soon he not only had all the chips, but he also had won back all his tabs that were in Angelo's safe. Angelo's boys were desperate by this time, and so they put the joint's total bankroll into action. They had decided to run a cooler. The hand went smoothly enough, with all the Dutchman's tabs and chips and all the money he had with him in the pot, and it looked as if they were off the hook, but on the final turn something went haywire. The Dutchman caught a card he was not supposed to catch and

26

wound up with the best hand. They told him that they were clean and wanted him to wait for Angelo, but the Dutchman only laughed, saying he had an important engagement that could not wait, and walked out with the loot. He had been gone only a few minutes when Angelo telephoned. When the boys tried to give him the bad news, he interrupted to say that they should have come up with a better gimmick if they had wanted to rob him. Angelo then said that he was late getting to the game only because he had been a witness when the Dutchman was hit by a truck and killed a couple of hours before and had been delayed at the coroner's office making a statement about it.

I do not know if I ever played poker with an earthbound spirit, lucky or otherwise, but I had a personal experience in the eerie department in which poker figured. I had been playing regularly in a private-club game in an old office building, and I occasionally used the clubroom for personal work in the early afternoon an hour or so before anybody else arrived. It was a large suite with one of the rooms off to one side. Several times when I was alone I distinctly heard the sound of paper being torn in that room, as if somebody first tore whole sheets in half and then into quarters and then into even smaller pieces. The first couple of times I walked in, confidently expecting to find somebody there, but since the room invariably was unoccupied I eventually concluded that what I had heard was merely some odd acoustic echo from the street. One day, however, I told the old elevator operator about it and he promptly turned pale. He informed me that a former tenant of the suite, whose private office had been in the room in question, knew he was about to be indicted on an embezzling rap, but before the law could put the arm on him he came down to his office one night and blew out his brains. First, however, he carefully tore up all incriminating documents and ignited them, but they had not burned out entirely. I checked the old man's story in the newspaper files and found out that it was the McCoy.

Whether I believe in the supernatural or not is immaterial. All I am sure of is that things happen every day for which there is no logical explanation—at least within our present intellectual

27

range. I have to go along with a character who was talking in a game one evening, about miracles mentioned in the Bible and why we should not question them. He said that when he can sit in his livingroom and see a fight or a football game at the moment it is taking place a couple of thousand miles away and not have even the vaguest notion of how it is accomplished, he will buy all the biblical miracles he has ever read plus any he may have overlooked, and no questions asked.

7
Amateur Night

There is a second sure way to identify poker-game weaklings (from the viewpoint of playing ability) whether they are novices or experienced chronic losers. They consistently reveal themselves by nomenclature. I am not limiting myself to the terms they use frequently to describe certain hands, for example, saying "all blue" for a flush, or to the corny synonyms they use in card identification, for example, calling an ace a "hickory nut" or using one of a dozen other fanciful designations that I have heard many times over the years. The fact is, I am thinking more of the other words and phrases that indelibly stamp the poker "square." Among the more common I would include *aces over* instead of *aces up,* and *a pair of aces* instead of *two aces,* to quote examples applicable to all other such hand values. Furthermore, these players do not *draw* cards, they *buy* them, and they do not *pass* when giving up, they *fold* (this is especially true in stud). I could go on and on, but a final gem will suffice, as I consider it the epitome of "square" talk—the use of the word *immortal* for *unbeatable* or *cinch hand*. Dear me!

In the interest of fairness I should hasten to explain that most of my long span of poker playing has been in public clubs and in other kinds of public or open games, including the ones in taverns and bars. In such settings the gilded terms are seldom used. The reason could be that play is more "deadly," but such usage is discouraged by the House (for example, on the part of dealers and other personnel), and the players themselves for the most part seem disinclined to employ the cute language of the friendly circle game.

I have, in other works, severely criticized fiction writers, the movies, and television for a substantial assortment of poker distortions, resulting in many instances in the public being terribly misinformed. There was one rather ridiculous although relatively unimportant miscue that heretofore I have refrained from mentioning. It occurred in *The Cincinnati Kid,* a novel about poker and poker players that later was made into a feature movie. After reading the novel (which I reviewed a bit roughly in another book), I was constrained to conclude that the author not only knew little or nothing about poker, but probably had never even watched a serious game in which important money was wagered. I could offer plentiful evidence to support this theory, but I feel certain that poker players en masse will agree with me when I state that this marvelous poker authority applied the term *kicker* to the hole card in stud. I have never heard the word so used but took the trouble to ask scores of players, expert and otherwise, if they had ever heard it. So far I have had no affirmative answer.

I am now impelled to state that the word *kicker* IS used in poker games, but never in stud. Its use is limited to draw. It is the card that sometimes is held with a pair or threes when drawing. Incidentally, the favorite designation of the hole card in stud by the Fraternity is *sinker*. Extending this a bit in what might be considered an attempt at Runyonese, on occasion a public-club regular might be heard to say of a curious but unethical neighbor given to peeking attempts, "He's trying to make my sinker."

29

8
Luck or Skill

I would not go so far as to say that those who believe poker is a game of pure luck and those who believe it is all skill are equally divided, but there are supporters of each position. Certain experienced players who should know better, or at least should rationalize more deeply, actually believe that in playing poker you win if you are lucky, and you lose if you are not. Conversely, there also are equally culpable, experienced players who believe that the good poker player will always win. Incidentally, nearly all fictionists do not hesitate, as a rule, to proclaim belief in the latter theory, and so contribute substantially to spreading the nonsense.

The luck or skill "issue" has on numerous occasions been the focal point of argument by attorneys in open court or in the briefs filed when the rulings reached higher courts on appeal. There are instances of learned justices of appellate and supreme courts pronouncing solemnly that poker is only a game of chance, and others, probably equally learned, judicially asserting that it is a game of skill. Some jurists have taken a safer, more logical course, ruling that, while skill predominates, the luck factor also is present; or, starting at the opposite end, ruling that, while luck predominates, a player's skill and experience might reasonably be expected to have a bearing on the result.

Cases of this kind have come to litigation, usually, in prosecutions involving an alleged illegal poker-game operation. It is to the advantage of the accused to establish that poker is not simply a game of luck, but that it is, in fact, a game in which the expert has all the advantage. On occasion the skill or luck issue has been overshadowed by a more material one—whether the poker game was operated for profit (charging the players so much an hour, or cutting the pots) or as a noncommercial form of recreation. Judgments have varied in cases researched as, of course, have some of the circumstances. In most instances, though, the operators have found it difficult indeed to absolve themselves of the taint of commercialism.

For my part I have to say that skill *does* predominate, and I have no doubt that the great majority of experienced poker players agree. However, skill is not applied in a mechanical or precision sense, as in billiards, marksmanship, etc. A four-year-old could be dealt a showdown hand against a fifty-year-old expert and the former could win because the odds would be dead even. In a regular game a rank amateur, or drunk, or wild-eyed speed player could win for hours, and perhaps could continue doing so in one or more successive games, no matter how expert his opposition. Improbable? Of course! In the long run, day after day, and year after year, the good player figures to achieve a winning average and almost invariably does, for the simple reason that he consistently plays with the percentages in his favor.

There are endless parallels to the luck and skill business. A baseball pitcher can establish an imposing won-and-lost record and earned-run average, because, in addition to his skill, he is the beneficiary of sensational defense; conversely, a good pitcher may look mediocre or even bad if the inferior defense behind him, while not making too many box-score errors, nevertheless does not perform efficiently enough to hold down the scoring. In football, countless "luck" situations in addition to a freakish roll of the ball can affect the result. Even a slight loss of footing for a split second can cause or prevent a crucial score.

In poker, good luck is not always the routine result of good hands standing up, and bad luck the result of having them outdrawn; nor is a player's luck determined by the holding of a long succession of good cards or poor cards. The elusive factor goes

31

deeper. Both good luck and bad take many other twists and turns, such as a steady player inconsistently staying in the pot (or passing) and related manifestations of the vagaries and foibles of human behavior. However, no player has the good luck or bad luck market cornered. In the long haul it all breaks even.

Acknowledgment must be made of the usual existence of an important psychological influence in any dissection of poker game luck and skill. Good luck will often expand confidence, improving the player's game, while bad luck figures to have exactly the opposite effect.

9
This Could Be Heresy

My position on no-limit poker (better known as *table stakes*) is not exactly a secret, but as a prelude to the observations to follow I had better repeat that, while no-limit is indeed a most fascinating game, guessing is its main feature. (Incidentally, *no-limit* in its original meaning, was just that; you could bet next year's cotton crop or any other asset, including the old homestead. *Table stakes* in the popular sense simply means that you may bet all your chips at any time.) To continue, the thoroughly tested principle that guessing is the main feature of table stakes is the reason I reaffirm that in five-card, standard stud poker, science indubitably determines the winner in the long run if the betting is limited. I also should add (because it is necessary for the accuracy of my rather adamant stand) that the ante should be a maximum of ten percent of the limit. If it is otherwise, especially if the ante is grossly unbalanced (fifteen percent or more of the limit), the scientific player is at a disadvantage, because he may be forced to gamble when he realizes that he is losing too many chips without action.

In the limit games there are, of course, player categories, but usually these are quite general in character. There are tight players, loose players, and the in-betweens, and all are influenced, in some degree, by whether they are winning or losing, as well as being influenced by numerous other possible considerations, conditions, and circumstances, including the time element, emotional pressures, inebriation, etc.

The situation in the no-limit games is vastly different. In no-limit there also are tight players and loose players and the in-betweens, and the potential of the intangibles mentioned above. However, unlike limit players (as a rule) what might better be described as *player types* develop. The phrase itself should be sufficiently descriptive because is implies, as intended, the manner in which the representatives of the various types think and deport themselves when playing the great game of guessing poker.

Nearly all of the no-limit types are more or less aggressive, and routinely include bluffing in their play. Respecting the latter, the basic theory is that unless it is known that they bluff, the chances are small of getting paid off when holding legitimate hands. Another bluffing dividend is that minor pots, as well as some that are not so minor, are won. There is a debit side, too. The bluffers sometimes get caught, and also figure to get little action from conservative players, unwilling to risk being chased out after modest investment.

Foremost among the aggressors are the blusterers, who make a practice of accompanying disproportionately big bets with an arrogantly confident attitude and a spoken challenge or gibe when apparently holding the top hand by virtue of an "over" card or cards, or small pair in sight. Sometimes these bullies will seek to intimidate opponents by resoundingly thumping their entire stack of chips on the table, or by dumping them in unceremoniously. It also should be noted that players in the category being discussed very often feud with each other, and delight in calling a disproportionately big bet which turns out to be a bluff.

33

There are certain unemotional players who will now and then dart out of their conservative shell and either call or raise a disproportionately big bet, or one that for some other reason seems to be an open bluff. Such players also are rarely capable of essaying a bluff of their own with a disproportionately big bet.

The rabbit blusterers also are a type. When such a player makes a disproportionately big bet or calls one, there are full stage effects. The gentlemen in question resemble walleyed pike and other blowfish, which distend their body to frighten off enemies or, at worst, make it difficult for a larger fish to gulp them down.

Beware the rarest type of no-limit player, the unyielding tight-wad whose bluffing is confined to antes and very small pots. He figures to win over the long haul because he bets important money only on cinches at least 95 percent of the time. He would be a poor risk in a popularity contest among the players.

The subject is so broad and, to some extent, so complex that almost an entire book could be written about it, but such verbosity would be entertaining only to a limited number, so the effort would not be worthwhile. However, one more word should be said about the difference between limit and no-limit poker. And it is pretty important, too. The limit game is infinitely more entertaining, with several players usually participating in the action until the end. And speaking of action, especially if we think in terms of a good limit ($2 to about $10) five-card stud game, the average pot is several times bigger than the average no-limit pot. In the latter game a big pot is an event, almost always with only two players trying to outguess each other. In the limit game big pots are fairly routine, and, because players usually are trying to draw out against the best hand (or representation of it) surprise endings are by no means uncommon.

Personally, I favor the limit game because, among other good reasons, I cannot lose at it—in the long run. And I do not have to do too much thinking, due to the method I have evolved. I can beat the no-limit game, too, in the long run, but I have become too lazy to be constantly on the qui vive, a grim necessity in no-limit, as I have learned on occasion, to my sorrow.

10
Literature and Less

A lady correspondent, exposed to some promotional material about one of my books, wrote to me in wonderment. She said, "I didn't think there was so much to poker that it would make an entire book!"

The fact is that there *is* so much to poker (and so little of it is known) that it would take quite a number of books to get everything worthwhile on record. For one thing, the jurisprudence of poker could fill at least two thick volumes, and still all the rules and regulations and requirements probably would not be covered. In addition, heretofore unheard of issues would arise as unexpectedly as they have from the time poker started. Let me hasten to state that I am not referring to the routine mechanics of play, but to the disposition of disputed points that may occur as a pot progresses, and to game policy. The latter involves such items as the check and raise, how to determine if a misdeal has occurred and what to do about it, cutting the cards, etc.

Another broad area has to some extent been explored by certain self-styled experts but not, in my opinion, even in a vaguely satisfactory manner. I am alluding to the teaching of the game, that is, how to play to win. The mere fact that a book is written for such a purpose is in itself nothing but cold-blooded arrogance. Now, I do not have in mind tutoring somebody on the mechanics of play, which any literate person could learn in an hour or two. I also do not mean the presentation of an assortment of basic facts about the game that will stand the novice, and also the unsuccessful regular player, in good stead, and may even provide a solid foundation for future development. What I *do* object to is the specious promise of triumph in actual game action. I will now repeat, as I have written previously, that there is no formula that provides the correct prescription for any given situation. The player is, at that time, strictly on his own. He may have been advised to stick to a high standard, to avoid serious competition against apparently stronger hands, to protect his own hand (when it is best) by substantial betting, to make clear distinctions between liberal and conservative players and to keep himself advised of their game status, to recognize erratic players, and to be aware of other points that are by no means unimportant. But, when a pot is being played the pupil is on his own. The teacher is not there and only the pupil knows the present situation and must act accordingly, using *his own* judgment. If he has analyzed the available data and makes his decision on the basis of what he believes to be logical probabilities, then he is pursuing the right course even if it turns out badly, which can of course happen to the best of poker players, including the rigmarole artists who have the conceit to claim that they can teach the proper moves without current data. And in each pot there are data all right, but by no means are they always the same or nearly the same. One word more. Whenever a player reaches the stage that permits correct understanding of the situation in each pot in which he takes serious action, he does not need a teacher.

There are still other aspects of poker that deserve literary treatment. Among these are history, personal experiences, stories and anecdotes of the past and present, the famous men and women of poker. So my message to the dubious lady correspondent is that there is enough to poker for a whole shelf of books, but with the likelihood, however, of the shelf never being completely filled.

36

11
Draw vs. Stud

Poker often has been called a very fascinating game, and deservedly so. And to make the sauce piquant even tastier, it may be served in two forms: draw and stud. (From my pragmatic viewpoint poker only is the five-card, standard game, and when I say *two* forms that is precisely what I mean.)

Originally, poker was played no-draw with a 20-card deck. Subsequently, with a 52-card deck, the draw feature became permanent. Straight poker, or the original game, got started around 1800 or shortly thereafter, the draw feature coming in a couple of decades or so later. Then, not long after the end of the Civil War, stud poker was invented.

The genuine poker devotee is charmed with either game, stud or draw, but usually has a preference. Both games are infinitely more entertaining if played with a limit to the betting, but also prove seductive indeed to certain players if the betting is unlimited, that is, as far as the chips on the table go. Somewhat prior to 1900, what was known as no-limit poker probably ceased to be played, at least in the great majority of games, open or private. This old-fashioned, and quite dangerous form of poker, permitted a bet of any size to be made, and if the bettor's opponent could not match it financially, the bettor won without showing his hand. It has been romantically recorded that in some instances both hands would be sealed in the presence of witnesses,

37

and the prospective caller given a specified time limit in which to raise the requisite amount, losing the pot if he failed to do so.

As stated (and somewhat boldly, too, as my opinion is by no means unanimous) the limit game far exceeds the no-limit or table-stakes games in fascination, and also (if the players are reasonably affluent and the limit is a relatively substantial one) in the average size of the pots. This means that several players are in most cases involved in the pot and not mere spectators, as happens so routinely in the table-stakes game. Further (and this, too, is quite important), the players ordinarily have a much lengthier tenure at the round table, because the absence of the "sudden death" feature of table stakes permits even the more inept ones to last longer.

But the primary purpose of this chapter is to discuss the differences between stud and draw. In the former, the action may be said to be two-to-one over the draw game, because there are four betting intervals. In draw there are only two such intervals, before and after the draw. Furthermore, the utter charm of stud is the fact that the mutations of strength and weakness may occur on every turn of the cards, and in the presence of all the players, in some cases heightening rather than lessening the mystery of the hole card each player has. From the viewpoint of the poker expert, stud is the one game in which his talents prevail, because he is able to make sound, nearly always accurate appraisals. There is, of course, no such thing as infallibility, no matter how expert the player, but his extremely low percentage of error is a guarantee of ultimate success. The limit stud game, it must be appended, is far safer ground for the expert than table stakes.

In some respects draw poker vies with stud in the area of interest and fascination. I would be willing to concede that, in a good limit draw game, entertainment and enjoyment just about reach their highest levels. I cannot, in all conscience, say the same of the table-stakes draw game. Of that game I say, BE-WARE! What happens after the draw can sometimes turn a big winner's stack of chips into a disaster area. The reason is the terrible uncertainty, due to the absence of any yardstick but the

38

number of cards drawn (if any) and, of course, the betting situation before the draw. As a good example (but one that acknowledgedly is not typical), I opened a table-stakes draw pot (we were playing jacks or better, a game I heartily dislike) with two aces, and three players called. Each of us drew three cards. I drew to two aces and made three, so my hand looked like a diamond-studded cinch. One opponent bet a fairly big amount but I did not raise, just called, being gun-shy due to previous unfortunate experiences. He showed me a *flush!!*

When I stated above that I "heartily disliked" jackpots, I did not mean to imply that the requirement of opening a pot with jacks or better necessarily kills interest. It is, perhaps, a preferable condition in a table-stakes draw game, creating a sort of safety valve. But in a limit draw game I believe that it hurts rather than helps. I believe that in limit draw the pot may be opened at discretion, with no strength requirement of any kind.

12
Player Parade

When you have played a lot of poker, especially in the public-club and other types of open games, you accumulate a rather substantial file of impressions that strikingly reveal adult human behavior. There almost always is a discernible vein of humor, albeit in some cases the engendered risibilities may be a bit on the mirthless, if not actually grim, side.

There can be no really accurate cataloguing, any more than you could catalogue the behavior of people in other specific activities, or in life's ordinary pursuits. Who among us has not encountered the shallow braggart? In poker games he openly boasts of his prowess, taunts and ridicules weaker opponents, and, when he is well ahead of the game (which of course is not always the case), likes to indulge in a boring patter of punishment for the other players. For example, when the hand is shown, he will not say that he *thought* an opponent had a certain card in the hole, he will say he *knew*. To cite other examples, he boastfully makes such statements as "I beat him to the center!" when he makes a good call of a big bet; or, if not called himself when he makes a big bet, he may superciliously imply that he was bluffing by smirkingly saying to his opponent, "You had me!" In the same situation (dependent on his mood) he may say to his opponent with an ill-concealed sneer, "You were smart to pass because all you'd have taken out of the pot was your arm!"

Some players are like certain individuals ever present in a business, social, or other setting, who would whip out a slide rule or actuarial table at the slightest provocation. A player of this kind will, if the mood strikes him, indulge in a display of arithmetical pyrotechnics by methodically counting the chips in the pot before betting, presumably to be certain that the odds are in correct proportion to the amount of chips he may decide to invest. Actually, this is not innovative, because some self-styled poker authorities, who write books about how to play winning poker, emphasize the importance of arithmetic in poker, a dead certain way indeed to stifle any latent ability of a newcomer to the game. Probably the best known author of a book about poker is much better known as an authority on another card game (the reason for commercial exploitation of his name in poker). He says you should not draw to a flush unless you are getting about five-to-one. Splendid! In almost any draw game you would have to be last or nearly last to act before the draw to be in position to know the odds. Furthermore, almost any player—unless the stakes are buttons—knows that it is not wise to try to make a flush if only one or two other players are in the pot with at least a pair or better. It also is not necessary for a player to have textbook instruction to realize he has little chance of pairing if he has an ace in the hole in stud and two other aces are showing elsewhere on the table. The only sound arithmetic in poker is reducing competition when you have the best hand, which greatly improves your chances of winning the pot. The arithmetic business also takes amusing turns. I recall a player once telling me that a reputable no-limit player had a great advantage in the game because he had a "photographic mind." As far as I am concerned, he or any other player could use an instamatic camera after each turn in stud and I still would not concede that he had the slightest advantage.

In some public-club and other open games in which I played it was customary to bury or "burn" the top card on the deck prior to each turn. This was done entirely as a security measure to keep it from being identified if accidently or purposely marked. Some highly intelligent players believed that this gave them the worst of it even though *all* the players were equally involved. Other players of similar intelligence objected strenuously if they were prevented from getting the first card in stud when the player on their right, due to a physical handicap or to some other reason, was obligated to pass the deal. The objectors had the weird idea that there was some kind of advantage in getting the first card. I have heard serious pro and con discussions of the point, but the logic of the contention escapes me.

In some stud games, especially those in the larger public clubs during the lush days of commercial poker, there was the requirement that the dealer (a player, because the "take" was so much per player per hour) put up the ante. This was an amount almost equivalent to the combined value of the smaller chips that each player would have anted. Obviously, this saved time and also avoided the argument with almost every pot as to who was or was not up. Only one problem was encountered. Now and then a player whose turn it was to deal next would find a hurried visit to the men's room necessary. In such case the House man on the floor would put up the ante from the absent player's stack, so that the next pot would be played with a double ante.

I like to recall some of the generally repetitious lighter situations in the public-club and other open games. If both players hesitated too long in a stud pot after a bet or check was completed when the cards were out, some other player, impatient to get on with the game, would be certain to say, "First man over wins!" Old-timers liked to worry newcomers by saying, "All tie pots go to the porter." These same old-timers would ask (not always with levity) a regular attempting to coach a sucker, "Where's your school?" Nothing gave the regulars more satisfaction than informing one of their ilk, who missed the previous day's game, that a well-known "producer" played and "put on a party." If one of their own booked a heavy loss, the absent player would be told that so-and-so "took a bath."

I played stud poker for years with a stout, jolly gentleman who had a quaint way of expressing himself in at least one situation. After betting all his chips with a strong hand into what *could* be the best hand, and after his opponent had begun deliberating, he would say, "The hesitation is lovely!"

This player's observation is not now, nor has ever been, in general use. Many spoken appraisals of poker-game situations and conditions were, however, employed regularly in the bigger, more popular public clubs in New Orleans during the heyday of poker, up to about 1945, and no doubt the same was or is true of public clubs, past and present, in other locales. Some were a bit on the abstruse side, intelligible only to the initiated. For example, a stud hand is being played and the high card, an ace, has been raised modestly before the first turn by a jack. A king calls and so does the ace. When, after the next turn, no hand in sight strengthens, and the ace checks, the jack also checks (at least in most cases). The reason? The player representing two jacks does not want to collide at this point with the "policeman," the king.

Some players like to refer derisively to an opponent who has paid heavily in a futile attempt to draw a case card that will match his hole card, usually an ace. They will say that he is trying to catch the "missing link." Even more derisive is the criticism of

42

the player who goes through with a hand even though his hole card, which he hopes to match, is lower than the "up" card or cards betting, and who is therefore trying to pair the "underwear."

Wrathful indeed is the player who has been "put in the middle" by a flurry of raising by two other players (this occurs most frequently in limit stud). Quite naturally, the player so placed has a hand inferior in sight to one or both of the raisers, but he stays in the pot because his investment has become so heavy that he feels he must go all the way, no matter what. When it is all over, whether he wins or loses, he likely will say, if the experience is costly, "They made a sandwich of me."

Many were the ways in which the regular players of the big public clubs of New Orleans, when in jocular mood, annoyed and harassed the floor men, dealers, and other House personnel, as a rule quite busy at their respective tasks. One of the standbys (to change the run of the cards) was to ask for a green deck or a yellow deck of some color other than the traditional blue and red. If the current House victim lacked anything resembling a sense of humor, and responded accordingly, the somewhat less than robust jest was considered a huge success. However, the demise of the gag was (if a weak pun is permitted) "in the cards." The manager of the biggest club in town was set and ready the next time it was pulled. He opened the doors of a wall cabinet in his office which contained new decks of a large variety of colors and color combinations. "Just take your pick, gentlemen!" the manager invited.

13
I Would Rather Be President

I had a secretary once who made her life a bed of roses. She never allowed herself to be vexed by such annoying requirements as verifications and confirmations. Her procedure simply was to furnish answers that she felt were proper and adequate. So if she proved to be in error on such occasions (which more often than not was the case, because she was a lousy guesser), her philosophy gave her all the comfort she needed. "So what!" she would respond to my gentle criticism, absolutely certain that her position was sound, "Everybody goofs some time or other, and that includes me. I ain't perfect, you know!"

Dealing with an intellectually impoverished secretary is, at best, annoying and bothersome, but the penalties are mitigated by one outstanding advantage. You know you are dealing with a woodenhead and act accordingly. You train yourself to be alert, always on your toes, dubious of everything she does, even to checking with your own desk calendar the date she puts on your letters because you cannot be sure that her calendar is not last year's.

Now, as I have indicated, bad as my former secretary was, you could "defense" against her (to use the language of football coaches) because of being forewarned. But what about guesses, exaggerations, and even raw errors that are encountered in books written by "experts"? What can you do about them? Even if you are yourself in the same field, and hurl corrections and con-

44

tradictions at the offender when next you go into print, the very best you can hope for is that you may have, in some degree, set matters straight. What usually happens is that a sticky feud ensues, with your adherents likely to be vastly outnumbered by the supporters of your rival, and your motives are roundly denounced. The fact that you happen to be right is immaterial because you will be too busy defending against charges of malice, spite, and envy to prove it.

All of the foregoing was engendered by some rather irresponsible statements in a book that I accidentally picked from a bookstore shelf quite recently. The author seems to have a big reputation as a crusader against crooked gambling practices, and has written and lectured extensively on the dangers of being cheated at poker, dice, and other games. The book in question, however, purports to be a guide for women who gamble, providing not only precautionary information to avoid being cheated, but precepts for winning play (*honest* precepts, of course).

I must confess that I have never been an admirer of the author, who could romp rather freely in a field of pseudofact, conjecture, and surmise, and probably never be called upon for cold, hard facts and evidence that would stand up in a courtroom. I also could never see much interest or fascination in the subject about which he has done so much writing and talking, and so I found myself not too surprised to discover that the book in question was selling at half-price. I simply cannot understand his unqualified statements, which are utterly impossible to prove, such as, "Twenty-six million women in this country play poker, as against twenty-three million men; 55 percent of all money wagered by women in private card games was in poker, and 30 percent in rummy." Wild, eh? Then he makes a statement that is not mere unprovable speculation, but a stupid and totally unnecessary error. He says, "Private card playing for money is not permitted by law in any state." He excludes Nevada, and also excludes California, but only for draw poker.

The fact is that in probably the great majority of the states there is no law against playing for money in private card games.

45

This is so true that the judicial history of poker shows, essentially, that the guilt or innocence of poker game participants often has been determined by whether the game was operated for the profit of the operator (i.e., was there a cut from the pots?) or whether the players were charged so much an hour for the seats. As long as the poker game, or any other card game, is not commercially operated, it is not illegal in the majority of states. The fact is, I am not certain that, on a noncommercial basis, it is illegal in *any* state.

So if the author is so far off base as the above indicates, how much credence may be given his so-called crooked gambling exposés?

14
The Things I Hear

This is not for the birds—it is for the women.

It has to be admitted that, in spite of the total fascination of poker, extraneous subjects sometimes crowd into the conversation. Almost anything may be discussed, but the things poker players usually talk about during lulls may be divided into two general classifications: women and other topics.

I think I have learned something pretty important from the miscellaneous observations of these socially heterogeneous groups. Nearly all men, deep down, not only revere women but are scared silly of them. The early maternal influence, whose keystone is respect, often lingers in some form. It also is instinctive to be wary of anything you do not fully understand, and hardly any men, even the boldest buckaroos, claim to be completely savvy where females are concerned.

I am just about willing to believe, after a thorough drenching at this fountain of masculine opinion, that it is the women themselves who produce many of the unfavorable opinions men sometimes form of them. Even the most insatiable wolves, unceasingly on the prowl, hesitate to make a pass without some kind of encouragement, direct or implied. This does not necessarily mean that women must be prim and austere in thought and demeanor. They only need a smidgin of dignity to preserve their amateur standing.

I also have learned from these enlightening conversations that men generally are hip to the fact that practically all women have a consuming ambition to get married. Men have subjected this to some analysis and agree just about unanimously that in her inner soul the woman who has failed to snare a husband figures that she has crummed up her life, no matter what else she may have accomplished. They also pretty much agree that this causes many women to marry for considerations other than love, the best reason of all being opportunity. Some of the characters whose talk I have heard say that the big compulsion to get married that women have is due not so much to their desire for such conventions as a home, children, and security as it is due to their ambition to show other women that they could do it. No matter how tough things are after marriage and whether they stay married or not, the sense of triumph at having scored is everlasting balm, according to some of the freely spoken opinions.

If women who are promiscuous only knew what men really think of them there probably would be fewer tramps. Incidentally, men make no distinctions with respect to condition or social standing. To them a tramp is a tramp whether she is on the bum or vacationing at the swankiest hotel on the French Riviera. Actually, men seem to have less contempt for out-and-out prostitutes, especially those in the top-fee bracket.

It may interest women to know that few men brag about their conquests and, when they do, do not often name names. However,

47

most men imply that they could say a great deal if they cared to open up. I have not found one yet to come out and proclaim himself a blank.

If judged by what you hear at the poker table, men who keep themselves posted on the current smutty stories are a pretty sorry lot as a rule, the least likely candidates for any kind of romantic interlude. It may be the result of a sense of frustration, but I have noticed that such characters—usually fat or bald or otherwise repulsive—seem to get a positive satisfaction from repeating sexy stories that put women in a degrading role. I also have noticed that the men who most enjoy stories involving crooked married women have little to worry about inasmuch as their wives almost always are grade-A frumps.

A lady poker player in a tough game gets to look the same to you as any other pigeon even if she is a standout dish—which usually is not the case. You can keep a pretty good grip on your chivalrous instincts as long as she is in there with somebody else, in which case you pull for her to win—so there will be more soft chips for you to get a crack at further along the way.

One night I was dealing and backed-up a fat old bag with aces. I called the first bet with a queen up and a nine in the hole and paired the nine on the turn. The lady with the aces caught an eight and checked. I took the play and got a couple of stayers, and she backed in without raising. On the next turn I made two nines in sight and she made two eights in sight. When I bet she just called. On the final turn I made three nines in sight and she caught another ace, making aces and eights showing. She raised herself broke on the hand, and when I showed her the fourth nine she said I was nothing but a heel for taking advantage of a lady, and she threatened to call the law. I admit that the hand looked like a grade-A cooler, but if she had not played her two aces weak at the outset to trap me or some other victim, she probably would have won the pot because the draw would have been different. She eventually realized this too, but if she profited from the experience she is no lady.

48

15
Hard Way to Make an Easy Living

The fabulous professional poker player who leads a plush existence made possible by handsome winnings is the beau ideal of all who play poker for a living. However, few attain this exalted goal, so most of us get to know only the average professional, who more often than not is looking for somebody to put the bite on so he can get back into action.

Poker hustlers (the word *professional* is rarely used in designating those who play for a living) may be divided into three general categories. The first of course is the smoothie who makes gobs of money at it by fair means or foul and who you see in the movies and television if no other place. In the second group may be placed the cream of the hustler crop, a very few top-notchers who usually play high-stake, no-limit poker and do well at it—at least sporadically. In the third, and by far most numerous, category are the two-bit chiselers who infest public-club and barroom games, and are happy if they make an occasional score.

The small-time hustler plays as tight and as tough as he knows how. He takes advantage of every possible angle, such as waiting for impetuous players behind him to act so that he can duck a raise if one is coming; ingratiating himself with other players including rank suckers so that they will not punish him if holding top hand against him; and in every conceivable manner trying to avoid getting hurt. When he can do so with reasonable impunity, however, he does not hesitate to deal out punishment. He

49

usually operates with a precarious bankroll and therefore is frequently looking for guys who are holding, or he goes on the House tab if he can or gets staked by the House.

The petty hustler usually is no great shakes as a poker player. He is lacking in flexibility, aggressiveness, and financial resources. He tries to play nothing but cinches, consequently losing the advantage of a logical spread of his play, which entails calculated risks but which insures a winning percentage—if the formula is sound.

The big-time hustler is a different breed. He is well aware of the disadvantage of short money, so he either has a substantial operating bankroll or can come up with new money on short notice. He likes soft action with its potential of big profit but will sometimes battle it out in tough company on his private theory that he is just a little better. He has a good nose for games to his liking, in his own community or maybe a hop across the continent. Wherever the action is best, whether it be Miami or Seattle or a dot on the map, he is ready to go.

Nearly all poker hustlers, small time or big, are also horse players and take other action. The chiselers take their action in these activities the same way as in poker—strictly small time. The big operators, if they like a horse or a football team, may unhesitatingly go for broke. One of these characters I knew would always borrow, when he was a little short, enough to bet at least an even hundred. He said he liked only round figures.

16
Blood and Guts and the Hereafter

One evening a poker player made a remarkably good call and won a big pot. The call was a good one in that not only did it seem probable that the bettor had the caller beaten, it seemed almost a certainty that the remaining player, still to act, had the best hand of all; but, unaccountably, he passed!

A friend of the astute player who made the extraordinary call remarked that the latter "had more guts than Blood and Guts Patton." He spoke with the voice of authority as he had witnessed many other examples of his pal's unquestioned moxie.

The cold truth is that the call was a piece of unparalleled poker stupidity. The fact that the caller won the pot is unimportant. Any second- or even third-rate poker player would unhesitatingly have thrown the hand away, and he would have been right. The brave poker player simply did not have enough savvy to realize that to call was not good poker. Since he played consistently with the same lack of fear—and judgment—he naturally lost consistently. Miracles do not happen too often.

Heroic deeds capture the imagination and win our admiration, especially if they are accomplished in the face of terrific odds. This feeling has existed through the ages. Gifted authors have penned untold immortal lines to sustain it and it likewise is reflected in the vaunted language carved in marble on many a proud mausoleum and tomb. Yet it could be true that deeds of bravery are sometimes just sheer foolhardiness that works, as in the case of the poker player who took the chance reason would have rejected. I do not despise bravery but I admire courage more. I regard courage as the overcoming of fear, not the absence of it, knowing the score but looking peril squarely in the face if a worthwhile issue is involved, determined to battle with all you have to the end, whether it be victory or disaster.

A pretty sharp politician of my acquaintance was elected regularly every four years to a soft, high-pay job no matter which faction won. He always was identified with the current administration, if not before election almost immediately afterward. He said he was addicted to harmony.

This politician thought bravery was a fine quality and also expressed respect and esteem for the stalwarts who battled for what they believed to be right, no matter what the cost. He said that personally he could not afford such a luxury because he believed in a political hereafter, a purgatorial state of joblessness achieved by disregarding the wishes of your constituents in favor of principle.

Since I started on this politician I might as well add that he also was of an extremely cynical turn in other respects. He scoffed at the idea, for example, of "incorruptible" individuals—public officials or otherwise. He said that in his opinion the rather depressing and happily unprevalent theory that "every man has his price" is pretty solid. It seems that he harbored the misanthropic belief that the reason so many characters get a reputation for incorruptibility is only that they do not get the right kind of temptation. He said that while they may not make a deal with Lucifer on a soul-bartering basis, many of our most virtuous citizens (especially if they are already well heeled) who would call the law if you offered them a routine bribe, might bend a responsive ear if the lure were something heretofore considered to be unobtainable.

17
Peccadilloes

After many years of experience and close observation, I hold the opinion (which I have expounded upon in other works) that there is relatively little cheating in poker games. This is especially true of commercial games, because the operators have scant interest in who wins or loses. Of course, anything but an honest game would be fatal to House business, which is maintained either by an hourly fee from each player or by taking from pots on a percentage basis.

When I referred to cheating I meant dishonest dealing, such as plucking a card from the bottom of the deck, or dealing the second one from the top instead of the legal top one. I also had in mind marking backs and edges of cards, and the skulduggery of running in a cold deck or cooler, in other words a fixed deck, an infallible method of cheating if the switch is made successfully. I also had in mind other forms of outright thievery, such as a player slipping a confederate a needed card.

There are other areas in poker games that lend themselves to more subtle forms of crookedness. One, not too common, is the exchange of signals between players (usually not more than two) to reveal hand strength. The advantage here is the building of a pot by an accomplice when his partner is holding a strong hand. The former, after raising a few times, will pass, feigning dejection at defeat.

Probably the most "innocent" form of illegal deception can

occur in stud poker. This involves the position of the exposed or "up" cards in a player's hand. It is a firm rule that the exposed cards must remain in the position in which they were dealt. Thus, if a player's first card showing is an ace, his second a five, his third a king, and his fourth a deuce, these cards must remain that way, because otherwise there could easily be a mistake in appraising the strength of the hand. Suppose, for example, a player has eights back-to-back and raises the pot rather substantially before the first turn (or when the hands on the table consist only of the hole card and one up card) and two or three other players call, including one who has a nine as his exposed card. Nobody helps on the next round of exposed cards, but the player with the nine catches a six and switches this with the nine so that it appears that the six was his first exposed card. Assuming that this was unobserved, when the cards are out the player with the eights makes two eights in sight and the player who has switched the first two cards makes two nines in sight. The former is reasonably certain that the player with the two nines showing is backed up with sixes or has a big hole card, so he bets confidently; but he collides with disaster when his opponent turns over the third nine when all the chips are in the center.

In a case such as the one above, the accusation of dishonesty will hardly prevail, if such a charge is made. The two cards *could* have been switched accidentally in the excitement of play, possibly deflected out of correct position by a chip or chips carelessly tossed into the pot by another player, or inadvertently by the palm or sleeve of the holder. It also may be contended by the winner that the other should have *known* which card was first, and should have called attention to the position change immediately and not try to claim foul when the pot was over. (A good player, who knows he must give full attention to every detail of the action, will be aware of a switch in the position of up cards if one is made but will pretend not to notice, therefore accruing to himself an important advantage.)

Still another dark area in poker is known as *angles* in the commercial games but may be otherwise identified in the private or friendly circle games. However, whatever the identification, the *modus operandi* is the same. It simply amounts to a player giving himself, by speech or gesture, an unethical advantage. It can happen in any number of ways, for example, by raising out of turn to influence a player on the right, yet to act, to get out of the pot; or, by pretending to be ready to pass, to influence a player on the left to come into the pot when he may otherwise have stayed out. Some games take a dim view of such infractions and may even bar a player who commits a second or third offense, but in my opinion this is a juvenile attitude. No poker player of any experience should be tricked into playing or not playing in a pot, and if he falls victim more than once he is in a category of gilded stupidity. The perpetrator of the shenanigan, as soon as it becomes known that this is his style, will not only reap no benefit but eventually will get the worst of it. In one game I know of, the raise or bet out of turn would be unrewarding because the player would be obliged to do exactly as he has announced. Incidentally, some stud players switch a big card up with a small hole card at the outset of the pot (I have only seen this in limit games when the action was fast and there usually were several stayers in every pot). Obviously, it is better to have a big pair out of sight than in sight, so the player can only hope that what he has done will not be observed. Naturally, I have not the slightest objection to such a maneuver, because it is indeed delightful to know an opponent's hole card, but, strange as it may seem, the majority of players who happen to see the switch will protest.

18
Nothing to It

I was in a limit stud game recently in which one of the players—
an attorney noted for his brilliant defense tactics—made a call
that qualified him for the knucklehead category. With no more
cards to come, a player with two sevens in sight bet and was
called by a player with two treys in sight. The lawyer, although
last to act, also called. He had no pair showing nor could his hand
have been a straight or a flush. Quite naturally, he did not win.

The astute barrister, a nimble thinker on his feet in court,
goofed completely in handling a perfectly simple poker situation.
In fact, when his attention was called, in private, to his wasteful
action, he could not immediately understand that he had blun-
dered. All he was certain of was that he had a pair bigger than
anything he could see and therefore, according to his lights, had
a call coming.

In *Life on the Mississippi*, Mark Twain tells of his frustration
and despair as a cub pilot when the complexities of the vocation
to which he aspired were exposed. It would not be an exaggeration
to state that attaining something resembling a degree of perfection
or even excellence as a poker player is a much more severe experience than that faced by the cub pilot. The trick with the boat
is to keep out of trouble by following the proper course. With
poker the trick is the same, but the additional trick is to understand that you cannot expect much guidance beyond what you
realize from your own ability to profit from experience.

The error committed by the sharp legal mind was not necessarily an error of judgment, if it is considered that the lawyer simply did not bother to project his thinking far enough. Had he done so, he doubtlessly would have realized that his one pair, although bigger than the original bettor's sevens, could not win because the first caller, with two treys in sight, obviously had to have at least two pairs. There may have been some justification for the call if the player with the two treys had raised. The lawyer then may have figured that the raise was a bold attempt to bluff, or he may have suspected that the raise was intended to freeze him out, assuming that the bettor and raiser were in cahoots. This latter situation is most unlikely but always possible.

Many experienced poker players frequently do what the lawyer did—act without thinking—resulting in costly mistakes that are not necessarily errors of judgment in the sense that they stem from thought processes leading to a logical conclusion. The major reason for this is the fact that poker is apparently so lacking in anything mysterious or complex that it is taken too lightly. This utter simplicity is the siren that leads players to destruction.

After all, what is there to the game? All you have to learn are nine hands: high card, one pair, two pairs, three of a kind, straight, flush, full house, four of a kind, and straight flush, which prevail in that order, royal straight flush being highest. Even if you are playing with one or more "wild" cards, the only other hand you can make is five of a kind, usually considered the highest of all, beating a straight flush. Some very few games include three or four extra combinations, but learning them is easily accomplished —just a little additional tax on the memory. The only object is to wind up with the highest hand, which entitles you to the pot. (There also is a "poker" game called low ball that reverses the order of things by having the lowest hand win; in most low ball games the best hand is five high, as straights and flushes do not count. Where they do count, seven high is the best hand because the ace is not used as a "one.")

The great majority of experienced players seem to take the position that, having progressed to a certain point, they know everything about poker that is worth knowing. They seem to arrive at the mental atrophy stage relatively early. The best proof is that after ten or twenty years or even longer they continue to play in exactly the same way, making the same errors and maintaining the same attitudes, and they are convinced that when they lose it is simply the result of bad luck and not poor performance. Probably the most important reason for this delusion is that they have concentrated on only one segment of the game, that which is concerned with the actual playing of a hand. Many experienced players are quite capable of playing a given hand, especially a good one, very adroitly indeed. This talent as far as it goes is not to be despised, but it very often is counterbalanced by significant deficiencies.

The outstandingly successful poker player is frequently misunderstood because he is given credit more often than not for what he does when actually his real skill is best exemplified by what he does not do. This is simply another way of saying that he has adopted certain consistent procedures including a high standard for participation from which he rarely departs, thereby effecting a saving so substantial that when in good luck he will win more than other experienced players and when in bad luck lose less.

The fact that many variations of standard poker have come into being is traceable largely to frustrations of certain experienced players. Having failed to achieve the success they undoubtedly felt was their due they laid the blame not on themselves, where it rightfully belonged, but on the game. So they followed the line of least resistance. They simply changed the game. It is interesting to note that variations of the standard game without exception increase the luck potential.

19
You Must Learn to Count

Poker is the only game I know of in which you may be disqualified for taking a little the worst of it.

If you play poker in other than the sissy games, especially the public club and nearly all tavern games, you will be required to conform to certain basic House rules. Possibly the most important of these is that you protect your hand at all times. In order to win you must show a five-card hand. Thus, if your hand is somehow fouled along the way, and you come up with more or fewer than five cards, you cannot win.

It is pretty easy to figure out why you cannot win with more than five cards, because obviously you have a mathematical advantage. The rule that you cannot win with four cards or less is not quite as simple. Many times you could win with only two cards, if they happened to be a pair or high card combination bigger than anything in your opponent's five cards. This rule, however, is inflexible. If you wind up with four aces but only four cards and your opponent has five cards and cannot even beat one ace, you lose by disqualification.

I have spent a lot of time trying to run down the reason for the rule. The best answer I can get from game operators and the most experienced players is that it takes five cards to make a hand, therefore anything less is simply no hand and accordingly cannot be considered. The fact that you may be willing to play with the reduced number, and the additional fact that you thoroughly understand that you cannot hope to make a straight or a flush gets you nowhere. Five cards make a hand; five cards you must have.

The chances are that the primary object of the rule is to eliminate confusion and collusion. Since the players know that unless they have five cards they cannot win, they are likely to keep a sharper watch on their hands while the deal is in progress and otherwise. The fact that fumbling or carelessness might cost them a pot is a pretty good incentive to orderly proceedings. On the collusion angle, the rule holds down the possibility of cheaters slipping their partners a needed card. There are at least two reasons for this. The cheater who gets help may need his partner to drive the play for him and then pass, which would be impossible because the partner automatically would be out of action for having an improper number of cards. (Incidentally, the disqualification occurs at any stage of the play if it is discovered that a player is a card short, and he loses whatever he may have put into the pot.) The other reason is that even if a cheater helps his partner he may want to stay in action for insurance, in case the fall of the cards should make his hand the one to beat. Since he needs five cards to win, this would not work. If the partners simply had swapped cards, their hands would be legal numerically, therefore the four-card issue would not exist. However, it is a bit easier for one partner to get rid of a card and have another passed to him than it is to make a swap.

A wise guy I talked with about the five-card rule wanted to know what would happen if two players wound up head-to-head, and one had six cards and the other four. The House undoubtedly would declare it no pot and everybody would get his money back, but I think the best thing to do in a case like that is to shoot the dealer.

20
Disconnect Your Hearing Aid

One evening a poker club dealer buttonholed me as I was leaving and asked me to save his life by staking him to a sawbuck. He had invested the gas and light-bill money on a hot horse that turned out to be a stiff, and he was afraid to go home. I hardly knew the guy, but I recognized real desperation and gave him a break. He eventually paid off but later showed his appreciation in a peculiar fashion. He happened to come into the dealer's box early one morning just as I was remarking consolingly to a player in bad luck that the crummy dealers on the late watch should deal only in Alcatraz. This innocent generalization got me a rough panning that even deaf people in the next block could hear. I would have done something about it except that violence is contrary to my principles, and I also happened to remember that the dealer had a reputation for finishing better than second in barroom brawls. The house man in charge of the watch saved the day by apologizing to the dealer and transferring him to another game to cool out. It was tougher at that time to get dealers than players.

The business of doing people favors is a losing game, almost any way you play it. When you lend, the best you can hope for, as a rule, is to get your money back. The recipient of your good will, after the ephemeral glow of gratitude, may bear a secret, perhaps subconscious, resentment because you have put him under an obligation. You might eventually even feel a little ill at ease

61

yourself, with the consciousness that having done a favor you must guard against seeming to want some advantage from it. If you refuse to stand for the bite chances are you are put down as a first-class heel.

I once knew a solid millionaire who gave more thought to turning loose a buck than I did—which may have had something to do with the fact that he kept on being a millionaire—and he had any number of customers for touches. He said he went the route a couple of times for trusted friends when he was young and foolish but pulled up because he was allergic to getting trimmed. He said he learned how to say no in a dozen languages, except only when he knew that he had a strangle-hold on the borrowers. To these he would suggest that they apply for a loan to the bank of which he was a director, with the understanding that they could count on him to plug the loan. To refuse would look bad, so they had to go that route, zooming interest rate and all. He told me he got a lot of business for the bank that way.

It is almost impossible to avoid lending money now and then if you play poker a lot. The percentage is against you. As a matter of policy you do not lend, no exceptions, but sooner or later sentiment makes you forget policy and you are hooked. I have even found myself lending money to hapless players who did not ask. The sensible attitude when you make these loans is to figure that it is so much money thrown in the sewer because you are colliding with another percentage deal, lopsided against you.

Aside from a loan about the only legitimate favor anybody can ask of you is something that affects you personally, such as putting you to a lot of trouble or maybe causing you to obligate yourself to others. When you are asked to do something that involves some kind of unfair advantage for the beneficiary you are being insulted. Probably not many politicians will agree with this theory, which is understandable, because if it has any merit they are insulting people and being insulted every day including Sundays and holidays.

Sometimes the smartest thing you can do is to let people believe that they have got to go the favor route to get something done. There was a kind and gentle old lady, a friend of my mother's long before I was born, who was aware that the job I was in put me in the position of doing something for somebody in whom she was deeply interested. She spoke to me about it, and after checking the record I happily informed her that her friend was next in line for consideration. It unfortunately happened that there was an unusual delay. This prompted the old lady to inform me that she knew somebody else who had influence with one of my board members and intended appealing to him. I assured her that this was unnecessary, since not even a board member could improve on a number one position. She took my word for it but a couple of weeks later got impatient and telephoned to say that the board member was being contacted that day. The following day the old lady's friend got her turn at last in the natural course of events, but this did not keep the dear old soul from believing that I had maliciously thwarted her for as long as I could. She died not long afterward, and people whom she had considered to be heels were not remembered in her will.

In my book, the worst thing of all about doing favors is being thanked. If you can think beyond inanities in such a situation you are a genius.

21
Any Number Can Play

Many citizens are shocked at such things as the national lottery of Mexico or the fact that in England doing business with book-makers is legal.

For all we know, however, in spite of the absence of lawful sanction (Nevada and race tracks excluded), Americans do more plain and fancy wagering per capita than any other nationality. Even the Gallup poll and a dozen congressional committees probably could not come up with anything resembling an accurate count.

The rub is that, aside from the countless sneak establishments and solo operators making it possible to take action on sports events, elections, and other activities, people make their own distinctions between gambling and the sporting chance. You may recoil at the idea of putting a sawbuck on the line in a crap game or playing dollar-limit poker, yet unhesitatingly risk important money in other areas of speculation, including backing some screwball scheme that has the sanctified odor of a business investment.

Americans are resourceful, if nothing else, so we have developed a quaint way of remaining shocked at national lotteries and other legal forms of gambling while merrily indulging ourselves a hundred times and more every year in our own national lotteries. We may, merely by purchasing products for which we have usually little use, buy a ticket in a big so-called contest that spews out as prizes cash amounts as high as fifty thousand dollars, oil wells, automobiles, trips around the world, and a miscellaneous assortment of lesser prizes, including such trifling items as motorboats, electric refrigerators, television sets, and the like.

It once could be argued that skill, not chance, was the determining factor in winning prizes in these lotteries that are advertised as contests for the purpose of respectability. So you had to be of a scientific turn of mind or a Phi Beta Kappa so you could write the last line of a jingle, or say in twenty-five words or less why you liked a certain brand of toothpaste or gasoline. There also were variations, such as figuring out tough puzzles that would not have put your ten-year-old kid sister in much of a sweat.

It also may be argued that you did not buy a ticket, as you would for a lottery, you bought something in a box or tube or wrapper or can, and the label was all you needed to file your entry. Having at times been knee-deep in cereals, canned fruit, perfumed soap, and assorted other staples, and knowing of many others who had taken the same route, I cannot sell myself on the idea that we simply had an unexplained yen for items that we usually bought anyhow but now wanted to stockpile. Sometimes there were divergences. I ran into a starchy bluenose in a supermarket during this period, and noticed that he was putting a dozen cans of dog food into his cart. I did not know that he was a dog lover, so I asked him how many dogs he had. He said he did not own any dogs, but wanted the labels on the cans to get into a big contest. I resisted the temptation to inform him that the dog-food labels were the same as so many lottery tickets. I do not think he would have understood, because he was a stupid sort of old goat and there was no sense in needlessly making an enemy; but the temptation was strong, because he would have thrown up his hands in pious horror if somebody so much as mentioned poker.

There has been an alteration to some extent of the modus operandi of the national "lottery," but only to make it easier than ever to enter—for a slight consideration, purchase of the sponsor's product. You no longer have to bother with twenty-five words or less or complete jingles. Now and then the free doings actually are free, if you do not mind being harassed by cheeky automobile salesmen after you enter a giveaway contest by signing your name and address at an automobile agency. Newspapers get into the act with fantastically easy crossword puzzles, entries printed in the paper, and football-score guessing in the same manner. The idea is circulation bulge, to permit bulge in advertising rates.

Nobody in his right mind favors gambling as a steady diet, any more than he thinks lushes are useful members of society. So, in defense of poker players, who on occasion are unjustly maligned, it must be said that they would not risk the rent money trying to catch a case card or drawing to an inside straight, and consequently are not gamblers (in the offensive sense) any more than social drinkers are candidates for Alcoholics Anonymous.

22
Even as You and I

The chances are that the majority of individuals who get testimonials or loving cups for civic or philanthropic activities while living, or eulogistic editorials in the newspapers after death, deserve them.

Among lesser people you find the same sort of thing, but on a more modest scale because the individuals are humbler or are known only to a limited circle of friends and acquaintances. Nevertheless, while living and frequently afterward, the compliments flow because only good is said of them, and their memories are finally enshrined in an aura of blamelessness and reverence.

Poker players who are looked up to more than any others—at least by some of us—are those who remain their sweet, unassuming selves no matter what. You have to admire players who are always unruffled, always undisturbed by bad luck, always well heeled, who never ask favors or seek quarter, gracious when you beat them and, more important, equally gracious when they beat you.

When you hear of players of this superb breed passing on or perhaps being forced into retirement by some physical handicap, you usually recall your past associations with pleasure. As a matter of fact you might even feel in the panegyric mood (mingled with some regret) if it chanced that the particular individual was one of your favorite victims. Notwithstanding, you are willing to proclaim to the world the virtues and attributes of the departed.

Some historians have the unhappy faculty of probing more deeply into events of a preceding period than the contemporary writers of that period; or perhaps they have greater opportunity for unearthing or emphasizing certain hitherto little-known facts, which sometimes results in destroying or at least sullying to some extent cherished illusions about famous people. It may be said that none of the giants who have come down through the ages has escaped the ravages of such minute inquiry, so finally we are able not only to see them in their greatness but also to view their defects. Even such renowned conquerors as Alexander and Napoleon were not guiltless of military mistakes. So we have to assume that lesser personages, whether they be pillars of the community or affable poker players, likewise would shrink somewhat if exposed to the pitiless scrutiny of disinterested investigation, and we rejoice in the fact that their comparative obscurity in most cases eliminates this inevitable result.

An ancient hustler of philosophical turn used to say that you cannot really judge people until you see how they act when the squeeze is on. He took an opaque view of philanthropists and other do-gooders when measured in terms of actual self-sacrifice, and similarly regarded those poker players whose financial stability, compared to the great majority of other players, more or less made it possible for them to take good luck or bad equally in stride.

He was of course nothing but a cynical humbug, believing as he did that true character oozes forth only under the stress of adversity, and that many revered persons living and dead who were never really tested by life's stern trials may have been grade-A heels deep down. Once or twice he called my attention to players who had gone along for years serene and unperturbed, but who finally began to exhibit reactions normal to most of us. It was the old hustler's theory that their reservoir was running dry, and that they were at last "beginning to feel it."

23
Laundrymen

Before I had ever heard of brainwashing I saw it done in poker games. Naturally I did not think of it as brainwashing, but I did realize that there were boobs who let themselves get all twisted in their thinking because of some other guy's persistent patter.

Poker players ordinarily do not pay much attention to what their opponents say. Nearly all players—not excluding even the sorriest pigeons—are wised up on the principle that you should never believe a poker player no matter what. So they usually disregard what they hear, or they assume that the opposite figures to be the truth.

There are certain players, however, who work so hard at it that they manage to get through to susceptible idiots and influence them to the point that they feel they are chosen opponents and have a sort of obligation to give battle whenever challenged. The villain of the piece either steams up the victim by constant needling or manages to convince him that there is a guarantee of loose action every time they collide. What finally happens is that the sucker gets in so deep that he cannot back off and, instead of ducking the character who keeps racking him up, actually takes out after him.

Some players who attempt to brainwash you try an approach that depends for success on a verbally aggressive, often offensive, attitude. When you beat them, even though they may have knocked you off repeatedly, they give you a hard time with a steady diet of the "you're too strong" or "too tight" routine. After a while you begin to develop what amounts to a guilt complex and find yourself almost hoping that you will be lucky enough not to win from them any more.

There are certain players who contrive to do a brainwashing job on themselves with no outside help at all. They will sell themselves an idea—for example that their best chance of winning is when the pace of the game is fast—so they will start driving the play, usually at severe cost. Part of their theory is that other players, caught in the fast action, will get hooked with them, which they consider—not too illogically—to be good medicine for a game whose ailment is tightness.

Fixations in the minds of some players, which take root as the result of brainwashing by autosuggestion rather than direct application, are passed along to other players who likewise may become infected. Thus are created legends of invincibility concerning certain players, as well as other not necessarily well-founded beliefs.

I was playing for the first time in a soft game one evening and eventually only five of us remained, including an old-time hustler who was nothing but a mediocre tightwad from whom I had absolutely nothing to fear. Yet the House man in charge of the game buttonholed me outside the dressing room—unquestionably as a friendly gesture—and advised me to quit while I was ahead, because he was of the opinion that the old hustler had too much class and would wind up with the chips. The House man had done such a thorough brainwashing job on himself that he was convinced that a brash newcomer would have to be overpowered eventually by the veteran.

24
Mein Host

The protocol and other problems of harried Washington hostesses very often would take a back seat when compared to the wringer you figure to be put through trying to arrange the average private poker game. A poker party is something else again, because to this are invited, as a rule, couples, and there is the bait of free doings in the food and drink department besides the prospect of the latest gossip; but a poker game is a gathering for the express purpose of knocking heads in a fascinating contest of skill and psychology and from which, under sane conditions, women are rigidly barred.

Unless you are a bachelor, or the family is away, or due to the isolation of the game in a basement or a garage or some other location distinctly apart from the dwelling, where privacy is assured, you play under a twofold handicap. There is the constant possibility of the players annoying other members of your family who may be enjoying television or trying to read or sleep. Even more important, your family may annoy the players by unreasonable movements, such as putting out the garbage can or going to the kitchen or to the bathroom or taking the dog for a walk.

However, the number one project is to line up your players. You start off with a list of possibles three or four days or maybe a week in advance. Almost everybody you call is interested, but uncertain. Things look pretty good right now but they will not know for sure for a couple of days. Of course, they are stalling. They want to play, all right, but strategy calls for delaying action. If there is the inconvenience of a wife or possibly other domestic obligations, time may be needed to set the thing up; if unencumbered, they frequently put you off as a matter of form.

Other problems occur along the way. The limit is too big or too small. Some want stud, others will tear themselves away from television only for draw. Somebody will play if a certain character is in the game and somebody else will play only if a certain other character is not. The date will not be good for some, and if you try to make a shift you will kill the deal with others. The most likely prospects are always those who plead a slight case of the shorts (which is your cue to offer to stand good for a stack or two) and the practical men who are impressed by the roster of potential players if it includes at least two or three tender pigeons.

Sometimes those you invite not only accept enthusiastically but want to bring along a friend. This can set up a ticklish situation. The friend figures to be a right guy, but on the other hand maybe he is not. You also have to be careful about bad losers and, even worse, bad winners. Unless the quitting time is specific (and even this does not always work out) you have to worry about losers wanting to play an extra round often enough to keep you up all night.

Even when you have got a solid quorum of seven or eight players, you may still be in trouble on the night of the game. Two or three reliables always show up on time or even ahead of time. Then comes the agonizing wait for the others. The most amazing things happen to delay players. They do not ordinarily have such prosaic experiences as flat tires or bum arguments with traffic cops. They are more likely to be an hour or so late because they had to help capture a peeping tom who had all the ladies in their neighborhood in hysterics, or because a moth buzzed into Junior's ear and they had to rush him to a specialist, or because en route to the game they were pressed into service as marriage witnesses for an eloping couple.

Fringe problems include the mess that has to be cleaned up

after the game, and the probability that your neighbor relations have been put to a severe strain.

I decided long ago that it just is not for me. I not only have given up arranging private poker games, I do not even play in them.

25
Tools of the Trade

In commercial poker games, and also in the more serious types of private games in which the stakes may be relatively high, the chips used are distinctive, that is, made especially for individual customer use. While there may be basic color similarity to some extent in relation to poker chips in general use, there will be shades of difference. The lettering, usually initials, or design imprinted on the chips will be used only for those chips. When chips are purchased on this basis the general descriptive term is *check rack*. Incidentally, in nearly all commercial games, the chips usually are referred to as *checks*.

It probably is quite obvious why sets or racks of chips are never identical. The main reason, of course, is financial protection, to avoid chips not bought at established value in the game from being cashed in by an unscrupulous player. Another reason is that each House wants its own badge of exclusiveness or quality, as an indication of "class," high-stake private and commercial games alike being crotchety on the subject.

The cost of chips, or checks, can run quite high, the type of material probably being the important factor in determining the price. There is, of course, the item of design, both from the viewpoints of art and craftsmanship. Quantity, too, plays a part, the unit cost lowering as the volume increases. Some of the more expensive chips are smooth, glossy, and just about unbreakable, a pleasure for even the losers to handle. In contrast are ordinary chips, made from inexpensive, brittle material, available in small or large quantities in the average retail store, even in pharmacies and the five-and-ten.

The cards used in the commercial games and average private games, high stakes or low, generally are of the same size and quality, the best known being Squeezers and Bulldogs, both durable and easy to handle. The commercial game operators have the price advantage of buying in volume, which also is enjoyed by some of the more substantial private games. In most instances the smaller games buy a couple of decks at a time over the counter, at retail price.

In some of the commercial games a superlative quality plastic card is used, but this type of card has never become too popular. A deck of this kind is four or five times more expensive than the standard deck. The advantage to the House is that it outlasts the other decks by such a wide margin that it actually results in economy. The plastic cards, when soiled, may be wiped clean without impairing gloss or stiffness, at least for lengthy periods. These cards are about the same size as the traditional bridge deck. The majority of players, especially the old-timers, hate to deal them because they are slick, unflexible, and difficult to riffle.

26
They Like to Play

Indestructibility is the stock in trade of movie cartoon villains and dopes. They get blown to pieces, dismembered, shot full of holes, and flattened out, but in the next sequence they are back on the job again, good as new, and ready for the forthcoming disaster.

If you were looking for real life counterparts who would even vaguely figure to be endowed with such ruggedness and stamina you probably would think of tough commandos, or grizzled prospectors who adapted themselves to the rigors of an existence among the crags and chasms of the Rockies and such other forbidding locales as Death Valley. You would not, however, necessarily be correct, because the palm for this sort of thing properly could be given a rather substantial number of inveterate poker players who habitually shrug off ailments and disabilities that would hospitalize or at least confine to home the average, normal individual.

No thoughtful public-club or tavern game operator is ever without a supply of aspirin and other remedies for colds as well as popular nostrums for indigestion, cramps, headache, and related ills. Players who avail themselves of this service in most cases are well aware in advance of their symptoms but figure, reasonably enough, that the House's dispensary is adequate and that swallowing a pill while playing is calculated to produce the same curative effects that result under less interesting conditions.

Players with chronic ailments rarely permit pain, ache, or partial incapacitating disabilities to throw a block on them as far as poker is concerned. Arthritics and stroke victims hobble in aided by cane or crutch, and the heart cases move more slowly than before, but they manage to show. Some of the latter, warned against climbing stairs, have themselves carried if the game is upstairs and there is no elevator.

In a public club one afternoon where half a dozen games were in progress an elegant old gentleman, whose ticker had acted up a couple of times previously, was observed to slide off his chair to the floor. He might have been deserving of some censure for not being quietly at home were it not for the fact that he had outlived his family and also a couple of doctors who years before warned him to refrain from the stimulation and excitement of poker. When the crude ministrations of a couple of House men did no good, an ambulance was called. The intern tried desperately to bring him back with adrenalin but it was no go. When they took him away it looked like curtains, but we did not know for sure until considerably later because nobody stopped playing long enough to inquire.

The chances are pretty good that the disregard of bodily frailties by nearly all habitual poker players is rarely traceable to a preconceived mental formula or self-discipline. It is more a combination of indifference and a reluctance to yield to the time-wasting business of being sick.

Some useful conclusion perhaps may be drawn from all this, tied in with the rather firmly established theory that sustained interest promotes longevity. Police who raided a public club in the downtown section of a southern metropolis not long ago would have done better to send for wheelchairs instead of the wagon. They scooped up a score of players whose average age was seventy-five. The nestor of the group was ninety and the juvenile a mere stripling of sixty-eight.

27
Birds of Passage

Often when something interests you, you wonder where it came from, especially if it annoys you, such as a parade of automobiles if you are waiting for a break in the line to cross a busy street. Seeing about a million ants in the kitchen when you come in to make the morning coffee also is one of the many situations that gives rise to the same speculation.

I may be among the very few who have ever wondered where all the pigeons come from. I do not mean the ones that fly, although come to think of it there is an angle there, and I also do not mean stool pigeons. I have in mind the pigeons who play poker and without whose presence this very fascinating game would be shorn of its main attraction.

Every community provides an abundant local supply. Whether the game is in the rear room of a tavern, or a club, or elsewhere the pigeons find their way. Some are fairly regular in their attendance, others appear sporadically, but it is seldom that one or two are not present to enliven the proceedings.

Local pigeons you can sort of explain. They have roots, as it were, so they get to know people and places and in this manner get the scoop on such matters as poker games and where they may be found. They in turn become purveyors of this interesting information, thereby creating a pigeon potential of ever-widening scope, because the business of spreading the word is continuously repeated.

76

What is a bit more difficult to understand is where all the other pigeons come from, the ones that usually just blunder in. They are not part of the community because they are a transient breed, on the wing. They appear out of nowhere, grace the game with their brief but stimulating presence, and vanish again into the void, only to be replaced by others and still others in a never-ending procession.

Probably the most logical explanation is that visitors on the loose who have a yen for a poker game mosey around and ask questions. I have done it myself in strange cities, the best sources of such information being taxi drivers, waiters, and bellboys. If you are really desperate and hit a stone wall at every turn, ask a cop.

Some poker games have outside men who buttonhole likely prospects in hotel lobbies, airports and bus terminals and steer them to the game, but possibly even a better device is the pigeon trap. This is no elaborate contraption that springs shut on its victims so that they are held fast and cannot escape. Nothing like it. In fact, it does not even look like a trap. It is simply a clever location for the poker game so that it may be observed en route to and from the men's room. The pigeons notice, they come in to watch—and remain to play.

Among the more intriguing characteristics of transient pigeons, not counting their soft play, is the fact that usually their identity and sometimes even their personality remain mysterious. You sometimes find out that the pigeon who put on a few parties was a wife deserter, an undercover G-man, or a tough criminal on the run, but as a rule you never know. And it should be added, you seldom care. The pigeon is a heel or a right guy in your book dependent on whether you or somebody else won most of his chips.

28
They Set the Stage

Some people use everything but a television commercial to advertise their reputation for honesty—when peanuts are involved. They are the same as the poker player who ceremoniously returns a stray ante chip to the rightful owner.

In my opinion the great majority of officials of the big spectator sports are on the level, certainly well intentioned. The exceptions are the ones who sometimes cause your faith to teeter, especially those who are at great pains to produce an aura of impartiality. I witnessed a football game not too long ago in which the home team, unbeaten and a candidate for national honors, was having the toughest kind of time keeping the visitors in check. For three quarters neither team had scored, but finally the visitors got moving and had a first down inside the enemy twenty. They gained about eight yards on two tries but were then penalized fifteen yards for illegal use of the hands or something else pretty intangible as far as the stands were concerned. This stalled their drive. Somewhat later the home team started to roll, and after penetrating deeply the visitors again drew a fifteen-yard penalty for another vague infraction. This resulted in a score for the home team because the ball was placed almost on the opposition's goal line. Desperate, as time was running out, the visitors tried some risky passes. One was intercepted and run back for another touchdown, icing the game for the home team. With less than two minutes remaining and the home team again in possession, the officials suddenly saw the locals commit everything but murder. Handkerchiefs were down on every play in spite of the fact that all the big stiffs were doing was running out the clock. However, when the statistics of the game were studied it was revealed that the home team actually was penalized more yardage than the visitors—indisputable evidence not only of the courage of the officials but of their unimpeachable integrity.

A favorite gimmick of certain hustlers is to put the bite on you for a couple of bucks every now and then, which they repay promptly. When they figure their credit is solidly established, you get the rush act for a sawbuck or whatever they think you will stand for. If you go this time, you are a cinch to get your money back—if you believe in miracles.

Poker game operators could tell you a sackful of sad stories about players who give them nothing but good checks—until they finally cash the big one.

Not many of us appreciate the clever language of the oath you take in court before testifying. You not only swear to tell the truth, you swear to tell the whole truth and nothing but the truth, which holds down shenanigans by characters who make a racket of having plausibility going for them. Perjury statutes would be pretty superfluous if the oath were less toughly worded.

29
They Will Simply Love You

The best time to improve your player relations in poker is when you are taking a good shellacking.

This does not mean that you should neglect any opportunity to endear yourself to pigeons or even those players anywhere close to your own category. Desire on their part to beat you should always be encouraged, but it is wise to be as nice a guy as possible and especially to avoid antagonisms, because antagonisms can pop in your face at any time with unpleasant results. If you are in a soft spot where the pickings are better than average, it would be nothing but economic stupidity to create player enmities that could cause the red carpet to be rolled up instead of out.

The player who fattens his stack off you usually softens where you are concerned in proportion to his gains. When he is the beneficiary of your disasters he not only is likely to regard you in a much kinder light than formerly, but may even discover that you possess certain qualities and virtues hitherto completely unsuspected. He learns if nothing else that you are vulnerable, which establishes a compatibility of no slight importance as he may eventually come to the conclusion that you are, after all, nothing but a kindred spirit.

In the process of fostering good player relations when the going is rough and you are getting hand after hand knocked off, you should tactfully arrange for the winners not only to enjoy a profit, but a triumph. No matter what odds a pigeon may have overcome, let him think that he outplayed you. If you finally decide that it is just one of those nights and the only sensible thing to do is give up, do not say you are quitting because your luck is bad, make it clear that the opposition is too good.

When you are in the grip of a losing streak you have a fine opportunity to create the impression that your play as a whole has been stinko. Do not do your bleating about the current game, because your loss can be too easily tabbed. Later on you can get away with a two or three hundred percent exaggeration of your losses during the bad streak. This is very handy when you are back on the beam, because you can then usually peddle the idea that you are only in the partial recovery stage.

If you have any ham in you it can be used to good advantage when getting shellacked. You can put on the good sport act and say things such as, "Well, this is poker," and "You can't win

80

them all," and other corny remarks as the pigeons continue to tee off on you. You also can give the *savoir faire* bit a workout, when leaving the game after rough handling, by being graciously nonchalant in wishing everybody a cheery good night. This goes over real well, and nearly everybody is polite and answers you. When you leave winner and go through the same routine, you are lucky if you pick up even a grunt.

30
Added Attraction

Among other useful information you pick up if you do a lot of poker playing in the public clubs are some pointers on pool shooting. You have an excellent opportunity to broaden your knowledge of this activity (frequently discredited in polite society), because in many instances the poolroom serves as an informal antechamber to the poker room.

I used to think that pool was played only in two ways, rotation or French pool which is enjoyed by awkward louts of my class, and straight pool, the game of the experts. In straight pool you have to call your shots, whereas in rotation pool you smack the object ball with the cue ball, and any balls that fall into the pockets are yours.

The chances are pretty good that you never heard of one-pocket pool. In this game each player has one of the end pockets and may score points only by knocking balls into this pocket. The players swap pockets after each game to avoid one consistently obtaining any possible material advantage. The science of one-pocket pool parallels that of straight pool—to play position so that you have another shot when you make a point and to hold your opponent safe is so highly stressed in one-pocket that sometimes all the balls are at the end of the table opposite the pockets of the players.

Another favorite game of pool hustlers is called nine-ball. This is a variant of rotation. As the name implies, only balls from the one to the nine are used. You shoot the balls in rotation. The winner is the one who makes the nine-ball.

There is always a pretty good crop of local experts, among whom are two or three standouts, just as in golf, tennis, and other games. Important matches are frequently on a handicap basis. In one-pocket, for example, the handicap player may need eight points to win, while his opponent may win with seven or six points or fewer. Other concessions are made, such as one player always getting the break. In nine-ball the handicap player may allow his opponent to win with the seven- or eight-ball as well as with the nine. The privilege of the break in every game also may be included.

Pool experts are just about as crotchety as golfers at St. Andrews about conditions. They will use everything but a spirit level to determine the minutest slant of the table, will scrutinize the cloth for possible tiny obstructions to ball progress, and, if heavy dough is at stake, may even get temperature and humidity information from the weather bureau so that they may correctly gauge the spring of the cushions.

Watching a couple of top pool hustlers shoot and maneuver is by no means an all-time low in entertainment. The only cheering sections are comprised of citizens who are betting one way or another, but a spontaneous burst of applause from other onlookers is not uncommon when a difficult shot is executed with finesse.

It is my recollection that the top poker players (in New Orleans, anyway) had something on the top pool players. The latter were sometimes knocked out of action by visiting cue artists.

31
Bluffing

Bluffing is so much a valid (and valued) part of poker that without it the game would degenerate in time into a routine mechanical operation, with hardly any more mystery than exists in bridge. A progenitor of poker, the game of brag, popular in England in the 1700s, was a favorite of daring and adventurous players of that period because a player would win a pot if his big bet was not called. The word *brag* itself, the name of the game, connotes empty boast or bluff. A similar situation existed in New Orleans, where poker was born in the early 1800s, the original game, poque (French for *bluffing*), eventually becoming poker.

The temptation to bluff exists in all poker players. The most expert, those who have learned that bluffing generally is unrewarding, may yield occasionally to the urge to do a bit of "stealing," especially if the pot is small and the bettor's hand appears strong.

Habitual bluffers soon become known to the other players, and so profit substantially, as a rule, only when holding more than the average number of good hands. They also usually develop the habit of making too many bad calls, their own inclination to bluff wedding them to the belief that other players have the same failing.

Under normal conditions, in the no-limit (table-stakes) games where substantial amounts may be wagered, successful bluffing figures to result only in pursuance of a proven formula. The two basic elements are proper staging and reasonable alternative. Thus, if a hand is supported confidently at one or more betting intervals, and the final bet of the holder is substantially larger than the amount previously wagered, the bluffer's opponent or opponents are likely to pass, preferring to sustain relatively small loss rather than risk disaster. The savvy bluffer is well aware that if an opponent is too heavily involved in the pot the bluff has small chance of succeeding.

32
Homo Sapiens

The human element is perennially present in poker, as I have stated elsewhere many times, but in this instance I am not necessarily alluding to its effect in actual play. There is, of course, a definite relationship, but I am thinking at this moment of behavior patterns and attitudes.

Certain old-time, sharp players, usually those who successfully survived the assorted (especially financial) rigors of public-club and other open game competition, will tell you that one of the safest ways to guarantee incredulity in poker games is to tell the truth. There is an axiom on which amateurs and the consistently inept players dote, and often quote, "Never believe a poker player!" Now, this is not to say that exaggerations and outright fabrications are not more or less routine in poker, their users more often than not the types just described, but these same individuals also are the ones most likely to be trapped when the truth is used as bait. So it is not too unusual for the bluffer who proclaims that he is bluffing not to be called, and for the player who says he is betting a cinch to be paid off.

There is no setting less appropriate for prattling than a poker game, yet there almost invariably is at least one player who wants to get credit for his marvelous acumen. Such a player sometimes is guilty of fouling the game by introducing various topics for discussion, no matter how dull or juvenile. This is merely annoying and certainly does the game no good, but beware that his mouthings do not take a more perilous course, such as indiscreet observations about the betting pace of the game. If the action is fast (and if he happens to be comfortably ahead) he may remain fairly quiet, but if he is losing he is likely to break out with insufferable "original" remarks, such as, "It's raining soup and all I have is a fork!" On the other hand, if the game is slow, he will comment on that often enough to convince everybody at the table that he is smart enough to know when he is up against tight players. And the results? In the first case the fast players may become aware that they are doing the sucker act by loose and reckless betting and pull up; and in the second, the pointed reminders will eventually alert all the players in the game that there is indeed little action, so greater caution will be exercised. This will make a bad game worse and even may cause it to break up, because the winners will want out and the losers will realize that there is scant chance to get even.

Innumerable human foibles are always present in poker, just exactly as they are in other segments of everyday existence. The cigarette smoker trying to kick the habit might have an easier road than the consistent poker game loser trying to quit. In the latter instance, as the smoker tries, he will take oaths and make pacts with himself (sometimes even with others), but only in rare cases will such expedients work. In lesser instances (lesser because the issues usually are not as important), players will routinely promise themselves to avoid serious investment in pots when they know they have to draw out to win; to quit the game earlier whether winning or losing; to generally refrain from senseless arguments and personal entanglements; and to shun other deterrents to financial and physical well-being. Then, having given themselves solemn assurances on the various points, they calmly ignore the moral obligations with which they have saddled themselves and do the opposite; but on succeeding days, and on and on, they futilely repeat the same promises to themselves, promises made only to be broken.

Perhaps the most outstanding reason why the human element is such a significant factor in poker is that the game is a great leveler. The strong and the weak, the old and the young, the Rhodes scholar and the illiterate—all are relatively equal behind their chips, the result of play determined only by skill and chance. It might be stated that the player who has no fear of running out of money has an edge, and I concede this. This is especially true in the no-limit (table-stakes) game, and this may account for the fact that nearly all poker games today are played with a limit.

33
It Isn't Who You Are, It's Where You Are

The chances are that millions of people have never even heard of public-club poker games or their informal counterpart, the tavern games. This is not too unusual when you consider that there are all kinds of things going on of interest to many but that are generally little known. I found out only recently that chess fiends battle it out by mail, playing several games simultaneously with strangers in other parts of the country through arrangements made by a national organization.

Nevada excepted, public-club and tavern poker games seem to be largely a sectional activity. Up and down the Pacific coast there is plenty of poker. In some Pacific coast states and counties, however, the law will put the arm on you if you play stud, but if it is draw you do not need a lookout. You can find poker games in the Gulf states, especially Florida and Louisiana. There are some games in certain midwestern and southern cities and communities, but in the East, particularly the New England states, most of the poker playing is done on the social level—in home and private-club games.

In spite of the fact that poker is the most scientific of all card games (because a thorough understanding of the vagaries of human nature plus an appreciation of certain mathematical percentages are indispensable to success), it is loosely classed by the uninitiated as nothing but a low form of gambling. This causes poker frequently to be placed in such rough company as dice, roulette, and blackjack and other games of chance considered by the bluenoses to be very wicked indeed. So if you are a stranger in town you might have to use the "Joe sent me" routine if you want to get into the game—if there is one.

Antipoker law enforcement in some places is only of the token variety, but it can also be pretty realistic, having such unpleasant consequences as a ride to the hoosegow plus the prospect of a tough fine. In one big city, where for years you took no more risk of running afoul of the law playing public-club and tavern poker than you did matching nickels, enforcement suddenly became serious. To encourage the reform movement, the newspapers resorted to the sneaky trick of publishing the names and addresses of players scooped up in raids. I knew a city editor who threatened to fire a police reporter for unusual delay in calling in a poker game raid one night, making it necessary to replate page one to make the story. The city editor ordinarily would not have been too annoyed, but the delay made him late for an important engagement—the weekend poker game at the Press Club.

34
The Best Teacher

If you play poker like a drunken sailor you figure to be an ornament to the game until you are tapped out.

The custom of sailors just back from a long, monotonous voyage to do the town probably originated with the Phoenicians. If so, these mariners of antiquity could have had worse ideas, the proof of which is that others who followed them through the ages, including their modern counterparts, have done nothing to knock the game.

The chances are that, if groupings were made of poker players by callings, seamen would head the list of soft touches. This is not too startling when you consider the fact that many pull out all the stops once ashore, whether it be in poker or assorted other fascinations. This may be considered firsthand information, because I have played with any number of them, especially during the war, when they were fat with high rewards from the risky business of sailing in convoy in the submarine-infested North Atlantic. Nearly all had had spine-chilling experiences, including being torpedoed one or more times. Their stories of drifting on the ocean in rubber liferafts, and other details of their brushes with death, invariably held us spellbound—as long as their chips lasted.

Seamen usually are well-traveled individuals. I knew some who had been around the world several times and were familiar with the people and places of many lands, yet for some reason the broadening influences that are supposed to accompany such peregrinations were as a rule conspicuously missing. I have related this in an amateurish sort of way to characters who travel at home and in foreign lands looking at scenery and taking pictures. My addiction to nothing but the truth constrains me to report that here again I have failed to observe the broadening influences which I had supposed would be quite evident. Instead I have found such citizens more on the shallow and superficial side than otherwise.

Generally speaking, poker players who get by the hard way (that is to say, by some kind of toil, skilled or otherwise) are somewhat less than accomplished. Frequently, they come in right off the job, many still wearing their metal helmets. When welders and others were making important money during the war, there was almost always a satisfying sprinkling of iron hats either playing or waiting for seats. It used to remind me, for no particular reason, of one of my late father's choicest bits of philosophy. He had a theory that all you get out of hard work is old clothes.

Probably the best way to learn to play poker is by playing constantly, thus acquiring knowledge by experience. The lack of experience very likely accounts for the indifferent play of most casual players, which may be proved by the fact that assorted intellectuals also usually are nothing but pushovers. The most luscious pickings that come to mind were in city hall pressroom games whose players included newspaper reporters, accountants, lawyers, civil engineers, and other well-educated and intelligent pigeons.

35
It's a Living

Firemen taking their ease or diverting themselves at checkers or horseshoe pitching may give you a mild shade of green, especially if you have to work for a living, unless you bother to think that they lead a sort of city-mouse instead of country-mouse existence. Their delightful periods of leisure are poisoned by the fact that in the middle of a freezing night they may be hurtling through the streets at breakneck speed to square off against a fire at a chemical plant, or otherwise be inconvenienced or endangered. So if you think firefighters lolling about ornate enginehouses have all the best of it, ask any fireman.

The story is a bit different where the "firemen" of the public-club poker games are concerned. Nobody ever calls them anything but "shills," which is what they are, but they are not too unlike firemen in one sense, because unless they are called upon to play poker they have nothing whatever to do. In this respect they have it much better than firemen because they do not have to play nursemaid in between times to hook-and-ladders and other gadgets. It also should be added in all fairness that there are fewer occupational hazards in playing poker than in fighting fires.

Clubroom operators would like to get by without using shills and in rare cases do, but they are pretty essential and generally may be said to earn their keep. Shills are put in at the start of a game and are taken out as live players arrive. It is not too unusual as a matter of routine to get a game going with all shills. They also are used as replacements when a game weakens, to hold the live players in it and also to have seats immediately available for new customers.

Shills may have a fairly busy day in clubs that operate several games simultaneously. Their tough periods occur when business is slow. The fewer the live players the more need for shills. Sometimes they cannot dope out a single race without interruption.

While shills are not necessarily expected to win, they are expected to hold on pretty tightly to their chips. They take as few risks as possible and avoid fancy playing. A shill in a draw game one day stood all kinds of raises to draw to a straight flush. He made it and won a big pot. He was promptly yanked out of the game and fired, the boss telling him he did not have him in there to gamble.

The prototype of a shill is a seedy character of middle age or older. If he is not a race horse casualty, he has had his bumps otherwise and usually is quite satisfied with his present lot. The pay is small, but many shills have pensions from some source or other, and since as a rule they do not have the inconvenience of a family, for them it is nice work if they can get it.

Shills rarely are topflight players. The average shill playing for himself almost always is little better than a rank sucker.

36
Musclemen

Even if we do not like to admit it, most of us take some pushing around as we go through life or make unworthy concessions to avoid it, whether the bullies are tough kids or tough nations.

Of course we are taught that might never makes right, and

history—especially modern history—has produced some note-worthy examples of what happens to ruthless aggressors. The rub is, however, that these unconscionable scoundrels usually are able to produce about a million carloads of misery before finally getting tagged, so we have got to be on our toes constantly to avoid being listed among the victims.

Poker games are by no means exempt from characters who heave their weight around profitably. If a somewhat less than amiable gorilla pours it on you whenever he gets the chance, your desire to retaliate in kind is often cramped by some frivolous reaction, such as the instinct of self-preservation. You may not go so far as laying down winning hands to him but you will think twice before trying such fancy maneuvers as checking cinches or other-wise outplaying a belligerent monster who will at least reduce you to a state of trepidation even if he does not resort to physical violence. Actually, there is little chance of getting clobbered, but your appreciation of this often is not assurance enough, which of course is part of the toughie's advantage.

These situations can easily become more than a state of mind. Timid players who ordinarily would take action frequently throw away legitimate drawing hands to avoid being mixed up in pots with characters who may regard getting trimmed as a personal affront. Some players (all too often productive pigeons) will quit a game rather than face the prospect of insult or mayhem, however remote the possibility of the latter may appear. Sometimes players who are not so timid also duck or cash in their chips, because they may have strong personal reasons for not wishing to become embroiled in unprovoked bum arguments that could have unpleasant consequences.

One night a rough-bearded ironworker, with paws big enough to tear a Manhattan telephone directory in half from a relaxed position, gave a player a tough verbal shellacking for checking and raising during the playing of a hand. It looked like sure murder, but the bear finally growled himself into a state of sullen quiet. It was my misfortune to tangle with him before he had completely cooled out. When the cards were out he had a pair showing, but the bigger pair I had out of sight looked like a cinch. He checked the bet, but I played it smart and checked with him, happy enough to win the pot with the least possible aggravation to the loser. It happened, however, that he had nubbed a cinch into me, so I got a pretty good going over for not betting, besides losing my dear sweet money.

The best way to handle a poker game bully the first time he gets out of line is to spit in his eye—provided you have a couple of Marines in full battle equipment handy.

37
Tweedledum or Tweedledee

You can easily be a right guy or a heel to any number of people who know you equally well. The opposite opinions are based on the dealings you may have had with the persons involved. Actually, most of us form our opinions of others in this manner rather than impartially. It is simply the ancient formula of what-have-you-done-to-me-or-for-me-lately. So if you are a 24-karat stinker in my book, you may still be a swell guy in somebody else's.

The same situation exists with respect to merit and capabilities. Not everybody will agree that the fireball who rose rapidly to an important vice-presidency somehow made himself indispensable to the firm's success. There will be those who will say he had nothing but luck or, even better, used good judgment in choosing a father-in-law.

When you play poker a lot you can be pretty certain that all kinds of opinions have been formed of you, and the chances are that in many cases even the best is none too good. These opinions deal largely with you as a player or at least with your poker personality, because it is almost entirely in this respect that you are of any consequence or even interest to other players. However, in some cases other players may bother to form an opinion of you as a person, especially if you are a standout character in some activity unrelated to poker, such as philandering or politics.

It should be no surprise that other poker players do not always agree in appraising your ability. In my own case I am well aware that for every player who regards my play with profound respect there are at least two others who think I am nothing but a greaseball who never runs out of horseshoes. Sometimes it can be quite startling when you discover the slight regard in which you are held, especially if you have put yourself in the genius class. One night a couple of pretty stupid pigeons not only successfully took after me every time I had a big hand, but also checked a few cinches into me and otherwise gave me the full treatment. I should have showed them my clippings when I first sat down.

Nearly every poker player eventually is generally typed by other players as good, fair, or bad. These ratings are subject to revision from time to time because many players are influenced by current success or defeat, as well as by their own ideas of winning play. If you make the same play a hundred times and it usually works, but it goes sour on a few occasions when you are in bad luck, it is likely to cause a drop in your stock in certain quarters. The explanation is obvious. Even good plays can look bad when you lose.

Since consistent winners do not figure to win popularity contests, it is not a bad idea to develop a modest demeanor. You would be astonished at the few arguments you would get by charging your successes to good luck and the shellackings to bad playing.

38
Tempus Fugit

The office clock watchers you hear so much about are only pikers compared to certain others, who have a vital interest in keeping track of time.

A quarterback whose team is trailing calls desperation passes even if he is backed up to his own goal if he figures that this may be the last time his team will control the ball. If one of the passes backfires by interception or recovered fumble it does not matter, because at this point the clock is as much his enemy as the opposing team. In basketball the team on top, when in control of the ball near the game's end, "freezes" the ball until time runs out. Smart boxers may be noted stealing an occasional glance at the clock in the late rounds so they will know how to rate themselves, and some also do it so they can turn on the gas in the final thirty seconds of each round to impress the referee and judges. In many other competitive sports keeping your eye on the clock may be an important factor in the result.

Having to watch the clock in poker figures to be a king-size handicap. If you start playing knowing that your time is limited, you are sticking your neck out a country mile unless you are lucky enough to jump off on top. However, if you hold nothing but bad hands or, worse, if you get a couple of good hands trimmed, it is almost a cinch that you will get more jittery by the minute and will by no means play your best game.

Just as in football and many other competitive sports, the

clock can beat you in poker, because the game either degenerates or dissolves due to the departure of players who have an obligation to time, or because you have to quit for the same reason. If the latter is true and you hate to leave a sizzling good game, there is always the frequently yielded to temptation to stretch your limit at the risk of domestic fireworks plus a dopey feeling next day on the job. You would almost always do well to resist the temptation because you also penalize yourself, in addition, by playing under pressure.

In some tightly regulated private group games the clock factor is equalized at least in theory. These games start and stop on schedule with now and then an extra final round.

There have been countless aphorisms, adages, and wise sayings written about time, but if you ask any poker player which makes the most sense he will probably tell you it can only be "Time flies" (when you are in action).

39
"Sow the wind . . ."

I lost a pretty good pot in a stud poker game one night because the player ahead of me called when the cards were out, although he actually was beaten in sight. This caused me to throw the winning hand, since I had no way of knowing that the caller could not win because at that point his hole card was not exposed. When I later asked the player who made the bad call why he did it, he said it was only to shut me off because he had it in for me.

You come across all kinds of mean, ornery heels in poker games, but this was the first time I knew of one to pay for the privilege.

As far as I knew he did not have any particular reason for hating me except that he was a pretty dumb pigeon and played frequently, so in the natural course of events I had racked him up time and again but had not even suspected that he was in a vengeful mood.

Sometimes players who have it in for you for no special reason, except that you beat them too much, like to get you in the middle when drawing against the top hand and make you put considerably more chips in the pot than you had any idea of investing. When they do this they are taking the worst of it too, but because either of you can win (such a situation comes up in limit stud before the cards are out) it is not the same thing as a player deliberately throwing away some chips to make you lose.

If you are an automobile driver you probably can match any other driver's tales of raw and pointless meanness on the part of certain drivers. It is not so much that they will drag you behind them at slow motion speed when there is no chance of passing, or that they will cut across in front of you without warning or otherwise endanger you or get into your hair; it is their attitude if you show the slightest resentment, such as a tough look. It is usually best to let the thing go no matter how high your blood pressure gets, unless you have a slight pull in your favor such as a handy crowbar, or your billingsgate is in good working order and an escape route is open.

Sometimes you can get into real trouble in poker games by simply asking for it, such as voicing an opinion about some point of play that may be in dispute when you are not in the pot, or by giving out what seems to be perfectly innocent information. In the first instance the player who is not favored by your legal opinion is not going to rejoice. In the second you can be treading on dangerous ground without even suspecting it, as on the occasion in a club game when a beetle-browed stranger of Marciano proportions made a bet higher than the limit. I was not in the pot, but in a spirit of misguided helpfulness mentioned the correct limit. Only the presence of several rugged House men probably kept me from getting clobbered but good. Of course I had done nothing wrong, but the stranger lost the pot and, being that kind of unreasonable heel, had to have somebody to take it out on.

40
Never Say Die

I was acquainted with a man who had an income of fifty thousand or better from a business he eventually sold for a million—cash. He dallied in a few other business ventures (not being old enough to retire), lost maybe a tenth of his wad, and then began fooling around in the stock market. He took a grade-A trimming and pretty soon had only a paltry hundred thousand or so to his name. He was persuaded to invest this in what seemed to be a solid commercial enterprise, but it caved in under him, and finally he was glad to take a job at a salary he once paid the junior clerks in his branch offices. Many guys would have been looking for high bridges by this time, but he sweated it out. He liked the game too much to quit.

When you are playing poker, prosperity may be as permanent as the loyalty of a female whose affections are deeply grounded in nothing but sentimental considerations, such as money. One minute you may have a big stack in front of you and all of a sudden it is only a peanut. There is always the possibility of winding up like the character who ran his million down to a goose egg, if you hit a bad streak, unless you pull up in time. When to pull up is usually the bothersome question because you do not feel it too much while your chips are going, it is only when they are gone or almost gone that you get the jolt.

There are certain pigeons, the kind you send a taxicab for if they wish it, who seem to feel a dedication to fast and loose action. Most

98

of the time they do not lose their chips, they give them away. They do not have to be dumb, necessarily, or even inexperienced. All they want to do is bulldog the game, make big pots, feel important, and laugh at the misery they deal out along the way if they get lucky—which of course can and sometimes does happen. It is only when they finally get down to a nub that they put on the brakes, because by this time they are also like the guy who blew the million dollar bankroll. They are playing to last because they like the game too much to quit.

One night one of these speedballs found himself reduced to one naked nickel chip—an ante. It entitled him to take a showdown for the total ante. The sands of time had just about run out for him, and he watched, pained of expression, hoping desperately for a reprieve while the House dealer inexorably shuffled for the next hand. Suddenly he brightened and called the floor manager. "Change the cards," he ordered.

41
Batting Average

A public poker club operator, who had noticed that I was in a bad slump, suggested that I do what golf pros do when their game is off—get another pro to watch their play and tell them what mistakes they are making. I thanked the gentleman for his kind thought but told him that the procedure was not necessary in my case, that every now and then I ran into annoying losing streaks, which could not seem to be avoided. This had been true over a period of 20 years or so, during which time I played every day, or nearly every day. The slumps were the big reason I could never improve my average of seven wins out of ten plays, not bad at all when compared, for example, to baseball, where four hits out of ten at-bats make a superstar.

The outstanding anomaly of my play was the fact that I looked very bad, indeed, when losing. This was true to a greater extent in stud poker, whether the game was limit or no-limit, because only one card, the hole card, is unexposed, and there are four exposed cards when the pot is completed (I am alluding to the standard game, which is the only one I play). I have observed, countless times, the thinly concealed disdain on the faces of other experienced players while enjoying exhibitions of my "stupidity." In the no-limit (table-stakes) games, because I gave up just about invariably in the face of big opposition bets when my investment in the pot was relatively negligible, I even earned pitying glances, and I frequently (I had no trouble divining) was the subject of deprecating gossip in my absence.

The point of all this is that I can afford to make mistakes, that I can play poorly with impunity, for the simple reason that my *modus operandi* provides an adequate cushion for lapses. To begin with, I play in substantially fewer pots than the opposition, due to a high standard for initial participation. This means that I either do not get into the pot at all, or limit my presence to pots in which I have the best of it when important money is to be wagered. Putting it another way, my opponents see what I do, but are not aware of what I do not do! I think I epitomized it rather well one evening, when leaving a game comfortably ahead after having been criticized for some "mistakes," when I observed, "I don't really know how to play poker, I only know how to win!"

42
Vanishing Artist

The professional poker game dealer may never become extinct, but there are few of his kind extant, and it could happen that one day he will be in the same category as the dinosaur and the pterodactyl.

During the heyday of public-club and barroom open poker games, especially in such places as New Orleans and Hot Springs, there were hundreds of skilled card handlers who earned a living dealing poker hands. This is not to be misunderstood as an implication of dishonesty; far from it. The dealers to whom I allude were just craftsmen who performed smoothly in shuffling and giving out the cards, and in keeping the bets and calls properly regulated. They also, in most cases, "cut" pots in behalf of the House, and settled technical disputes that sometimes arose in the course of playing a hand.

The pay of a professional dealer was not too high, even in a big establishment such as the internationally famous old Crescent Hall in New Orleans. But the deficit was compensated for in the form of tips from the players, that is, when a big or even fair-sized pot was raked in by the winner. Now, not all winners tipped the dealer, and those who did were not necessarily overgenerous, but the opposite of these depressing situations happened, too. Some players tipped the dealer every time they won a pot, and, in some instances, if the pot happened to be unusually big, gave the dealer a just as disproportionately big tip.

It was, to an appreciable degree, wise for a regular player to be reasonably generous with dealers. It ensured a friend "in the box" (which was something like having a good City Hall connection) and was, additionally, an understood proviso that your winning pots would be cut as lightly as possible. In my own case, on occasion, if I won a pot that it appeared I would lose, and the pot already had been cut heavily, the dealer would ease one or two of the abstracted chips back into the pile.

Probably the greatest cross a dealer had to bear was the abuse from losers, particularly when the best hand was outdrawn in a big pot. This may not have been as painful as not getting a tip when the winner of a big pot calmly added all the chips to his stack, but it did cause some extremely unpleasant situations. If a good producer who was a regular player proclaimed that a certain dealer was a "jinx," the dealer was kept out of the box in the game in which the complainant was playing. It also happened, occasionally, that a dealer would be fired for that reason. During a period around World War II the tables were turned. Dealers were hard to find, and a player who complained too loudly about the man in the box might find himself barred.

Of course, there were—and are—good dealers and bad. Players like a swiftie, who keeps the game going at a good clip, and does it not only efficiently, but quietly. The most annoying type of dealer is a slowpoke, especially if he is a "singer," one who calls out the value of the cards in stud as they fall to the players. This happens in private games more than in open games, and some such dealers compound the offense by substituting corny identifications instead of the routine value identifications, such as *window frame* for a four, *Blue John* for ace, or *Jason* for jack. Even the big winners figure to retch.

It would be inappropriate to dispose of this subject without some reference to the mooching dealers of the public games, in which a House man was present only to cut the pots and regulate play, the players themselves dealing in rotation, in accordance with the rules. Certain players of this type when dealing would hint broadly as the winner of a big pot raked in the chips, and, in the exuberance

102

produced by victory, reward often was the result. There were, however, exceptions. On an occasion of this kind a newcomer to the game outdrew for the biggest pot of the evening. In response to the mooching dealer's not too delicate reminder, the winner brightened in acknowledgment, bestowed an appreciative glance upon the dealer, and then said, as he arranged the massive pile of chips in neat stacks, "I'll remember you in my will!"

43
The Worst of It

Ancient and modern sages have solemnly warned against playing the other fellow's game. One of the old adages perhaps says it succinctly and pointedly: "Shoemaker, stick to your last!"

Some poker hustlers are so good at the game that they actually can make a living doing nothing but playing. I must hastily append that I am not necessarily referring to present-day conditions, but to open poker games as I knew them in many sections of the country, especially New Orleans and other cities in the Gulf South, up to about the mid-forties. Getting back to the really proficient poker hustlers, I specified that they could get by very nicely if they did nothing but played poker. But, alas! smart as they were in the public club and barroom games (which provided a steady diet of soft touches at the round table), they were at the same time colliding with granite walls by taking action on horse racing, football games, baseball games, and even basketball games. All they were trying to do was overcome the bookmakers' deadly percentage, even in the giddy gully of point-spread football wagering.

In other words, they played the other fellow's game. Consequently, the bums I knew when playing poker daily a quarter-century or so ago are still bums.

Trying to beat what the other fellow offers even within poker itself is a hazardous business, and certainly not recommended. I have had some flings at it myself, with deservedly disastrous results. One such adventure was peep and turn, the five-card stud game in which the player has four hole card options. He gets the first card down and the second up, but the following three are dealt down and he may change his hole card any time he sees fit. It is not only nerve-jangling, but a memory expert would be hard put to keep track of the proceedings. I also tried seven-card stud once or twice, the game in which you have three hole cards, and also discovered that it was not for me.

However, my most humiliating experience in this area took a somewhat different turn. It was a standard, five-card stud game, no limit (table stakes), and there was no reason at all why I could not be absolutely certain that I could beat the game, that is, over a series of plays make a profit. The fact is I initially did this, but modestly, because I came in stale as a table-stakes player, having played nothing but a stiff limit game for 20 years, and, in addition, I had a steady run of bad luck. I not only got outdrawn more often than is warranted by arithmetic, I lost heavily on relatively substantial investments to set up situations that would almost guarantee my breaking my opponent, but the majority went sour before the *coup de grace* would be applied. My dilemma was caused, in the final analysis, by the game dwindling to five or six players, finally to four, but the ante remained the same, ditto the obligation to bet, if high, before the first turn, and the charge for game expenses, deducted at the outset, also was identical. So there were handicaps to overcome. If you had a high standard for initial participation you could slough off $20 or $25 an hour without even getting in a pot. So you *had* to play, to *gamble,* which was a condition the others, not players of my type, liked. Oh, and we played with two decks, in one game with four decks, each player having a deck. It was, in reality, a frantic frenzy. I finally got sort of back on the track by insisting that I would not play unless the game was at least five-handed, and that only one deck be used. And I should not conclude without saying that during the frantic frenzy era (seven or eight games) I made mistakes by the gross simply because I was not thinking right. And why? The answer is crystal clear: I was playing the other fellow's game!

44
The Ante

Players in the commercial poker games almost always ante without prompting, even if there is no House dealer. If there is a House dealer, or if a House man is sitting in the game to cut pots and supervise play, he moves the antes to the center before each new deal commences. In rare instances when there is an ante shy and the position of the chips prevents positive identification of the culprit, the House puts up the needed chip, there being an inviolate rule that there must be an ante for each player. (The House actually incurs no loss because the rake-off system makes speedy recovery quite simple.)

The situation is different in the private, or friendly circle games. If the latter are of the poker party type, any pot in which all the players have anted would have to be considered unusual. As a rule nobody cares, particularly, the betting limit generally being less than a quarter, and the ante chip may be worth only a penny.

In the serious private games, especially the table-stakes games, in which the ante more often than not is at least a quarter, ante lapses can proliferate sizeably over a period of several hours. And who pays the freight? The players who almost never are shy and who are penalized, in addition, by the irritating knowledge that many pots are played with one, sometimes two antes missing.

Some players, to whom putting up the ante is second nature (the result of having played in commercial and other games where strict discipline prevailed), usually take it upon themselves to remind the tardy ones to ante. This is not unreasonable, and certainly should be understandable and, besides, is eminently fair, because no player should have an advantage, but it can become irksome to the point of exasperation. Certain players, difficult as it is to believe, have to be reminded five pots of ten that their ante is not up. Is it possible that such consistent fault is due to forgetfulness? Perhaps so, especially in view of the solid character of some of the individuals, but skeptics might be tempted to take a different view.

In my opinion there should be no hesitation in calling attention to the missing ante, even if the result is the decline in popularity of the self-appointed monitor. Misanthropic regulars of the commercial games (in spite of the ante omission in such games being infrequent) solemnly affirm that the player who makes a career of ducking the ante will eventually accumulate enough money thereby for a down payment on a house.

45
Cutting the Cards

The simple business of cutting the cards, more often than may be imagined, produces poker game "situations." In most instances the basis is unimportant, even frivolous, but occasionally a serious incident will develop.

It is a generally accepted rule that the player on the right of the dealer cuts the deck. It also is routine in the majority of games, especially the commercial games, that the cutting begins and ends there, unless the necessity arises for an additional cut. Such contingency could be caused by a misdeal; or if in draw the number of players drawing requires that the discard be shuffled and cut.

Now, as uncomplicated as the card-cutting procedure just described seems, it does not always work smoothly. Traditionally, the cards are square cut, the player doing the cutting using one hand. However, either as a security measure, or for "good luck," or as simple perversity, the cutter may take the deck in both hands, making several cuts. The average well-balanced (and honest) dealer will have no objection whatever to this type of cut. There are certain others, though, who will resent it, even sometimes taking such a cut as a personal affront, and there also are those who will claim that it is a violation of the rules and a time waster. If the contention becomes spirited, the sacred name of Hoyle is likely to be invoked by one of the disputants to render his position invulnerable.

The fact is that in respect to cutting the cards, there is no hard and fast rule in the average private game, even if the betting is table stakes. Usually nobody cares too much, and it is not uncommon for the player whose turn it is to cut to tell the dealer to "run 'em." In the commercial games the situation invariably is the other way around: the cards *must* be cut before the deal commences.

46
To the Manor Born

The character busily wielding a toothpick while he blocks a door-way may not necessarily be chosen by exacting people as an example of good breeding, even though his manners otherwise could be considered impeccable.

This is of course attributable to the innate snobbery of such critics. They are, unfortunately, prejudiced against various forms of inconsideration and indelicacy and even take the position that, although the culprits may not be aware that they are offending, this is insufficient justification for the annoyance and embarrassment they cause. Some of these critics are so bigoted as to squirm at public lovemaking or perhaps wax indignant at some other negligible transgression, such as an ignorant lout in a crowded elevator or bus massaging their ribs with his elbow while he coughs in their face.

Such squeamish individuals would fare badly in poker games at various times because they would have a good chance of coming to grips firsthand with any number of innocent little manifestations on the part of certain cultured gentlemen whose total idea of civilized behavior is complete consideration of oneself. So if in crossing their legs such players bang a neighbor's shins or improve the gloss of their polished shoes on a neighbor's trousers, they happily do not give a second thought to such occurrences, which have not inconvenienced or annoyed them one bit. They also feel that they have suffered no loss to speak of, should they chance to be fond of onion or garlic-seasoned food, if they make other players in their immediate vicinity cringing victims of this bouquet, which somehow does not blend too well with an atmosphere already reasonably well-scented, taking into consideration tobacco smoke and other odors.

As far as I am concerned, such situations require a philosophical attitude. Football games are sometimes played in rain or snow, and occasionally race horses slosh around in the mud, so if the going in a poker game is rough you simply must learn to shrug it off. You can always buy a good cigar for the player who is smoking what smells like a delectable mixture of rubber and old rags in his pipe, and the sneezers who may be too engrossed in the game to guide the spray may be provided with tissues. It is just a matter of being practical, even if now and then you offer to bust somebody in the nose if he does not stop using you for a bed rest.

Poker game swine have you at a disadvantage because you are trapped with them at a table in an enclosure. If you do not like what they do or say you can always go home—if the hook is not in you. If you cannot quit, concentrate on racking them up yourself; but if bad luck prevents this, drive them to the slaughter against the best hand at the first opportunity—even if it costs you a stack or two.

47
Distaff Doings

Lady wrestlers have a lot of appeal, especially if they look good in tights. It is also a pretty safe bet that it is no knock to the box office if the girls' softball league is more loaded with cuties than talent.

This maybe is as it should be in certain rugged exercises once considered reserved for masculine muscles, but it cannot always work out that way in other fields invaded by women. The lovely in science gets no special concession from an electron, and she likewise may have to battle it out on fairly even terms in assorted professions, including the tough upper level areas of business and industry.

Reliable statistics reveal that more people play bridge than any other card game, with rummy and poker not too far behind, and I would have to guess that more women play bridge than men if only for the reason that ladies' bridge clubs are almost a national institution. However, if they excel at bridge it is a pretty well-kept secret. All the outstanding bridge experts I ever hear about are men. If I am incorrect it is only because I am influenced by such negligible evidence as bridge championships usually being won by men, who likewise seem to write all the books and syndicated columns on the game. Offhand I cannot even think of one lady bridge genius.

Poker reverses things numerically compared to bridge, because poker continues to be generally a man's game, with most of the action in the back rooms of taverns and in men's clubs. This does not mean that the ladies do not give it a good whirl, especially among themselves and in poker parties at somebody's house when three or four couples get together for an evening of refreshments and confusion.

With few exceptions, the lady poker players I have seen in the cutthroat games do not figure to take home any blue ribbons, particularly in stiff-limit stud. In a couple of spots on the West Coast where you play jacks or better draw with the joker wild for aces, straights, and flushes, they do not fare too badly, relatively speaking, because you can get to play the game by note since it is about five percent play and the rest luck, so it is for entertainment—and the House.

48
If You Don't Know, Ask

There is a judicial axiom that ignorance of the law excuses no man. This should be paraphrased, as far as poker is concerned, to the effect that ignorance of House rules is no excuse for a tough beef if you find yourself on the short end of a decision.

Although the basic rules of poker seem to follow a pattern no matter where the game is played, situations that can become unbelievably technical arise from time to time and are resolved only by the House rules. If you are familiar with all House rules, naturally you keep out of trouble, but if you have not bothered to inquire or have not been lucky enough to be exposed to an identical situation beforehand, such ignorance can cost you a pot even if, believe it or not, you actually are holding the winning hand.

The legal situation can often become critical, but most frequently does in stud when all the cards are out. Suppose your opponent were to bet and you started turning your cards face down, but with no idea of passing—in many games your hand would immediately become dead and you would lose all rights to the pot. In some games you have the right to turn one or more of your cards face down—provided you keep the five cards in front of you and entirely free from contact with the discard. If you finally choose to make the call or perhaps raise, your hand may still be acted upon.

The vocal angle also may cause a crisis unless you are acquainted with the House rule. In nearly all stud games, if your opponent bets when the cards are out and you say you pass, you are automatically out of action even though your five cards are still in front of you and completely out of contact with the discard.

In the playing of a stud hand before (and after) the cards are out, you may say you pass to indicate a check if no bet has been made. But if a bet has been made and it is your turn to act and at that point you say you pass, you are out of the pot. Not all players are aware of this rule, which is very general, and they confuse the use of the terms *pass* and *check,* overlooking the fact that the former may be used safely only when no bet has been made.

The primary purpose of every House rule is to protect all players by minimizing sharp practice. If some dimwit makes a bet when the cards are out and his opponent starts folding, the bettor may throw his hand in the discard (thus fouling it) if he were not protected by the rule that nullifies the hand that is being folded. The same thing could happen if some wise character has the right to say he passes after a bet is made, and then can get into action again after the winning hand is impulsively thrown away.

Sometimes situations develop that are not specifically covered by the rules, in which case the House representative does the best he can to make a good decision, always unpopular with the loser.

112

One evening in a limit stud game a lush was high when the cards were out, but instead of betting he turned his cards face down, and was about to throw the hand in when he was stopped by one of the other players. His opponent, who interpreted the lush's action as a token of surrender, threw his hand in the discard and reached for the pot, which now also was claimed by the lush, who meanwhile had put his hand back in action. The player who threw his hand away acted too hastily, and the lush, by his indication of surrender, did his best to put himself beyond the pale of the law. If I had been the House man when that tangle came up I would have asked for annual leave, starting immediately. My recollection is that the matter was settled to the dissatisfaction of both players by splitting the pot. My own opinion is that the lush was out of action because he turned his cards face down. All the other player had to do was hold his hand and await the House decision, which then unquestionably would have been in his favor.

49
Admission Free

The two-fisted heroes of television and the movies, who slug it out with the bad guys in the brawl sequences, make it look so convincing that you sometimes wonder how they can even stand up under the exercise. It can wear you out just watching them taking turns knocking each other down.

If you have never seen the real article, you have not missed too much, because the make-believe comes pretty close to what actually happens when a couple of tough citizens tie up in a barroom. About all you do not see is the mess they usually make of each other.

When a fight starts in a poker game your first concern is for your chips. There is always the chance that the table will be bumped hard or even tipped over, in which case (unless you have stuffed your chips in your pockets) it is a pretty safe bet that you will wind up with a short count. If the action commences so unexpectedly that you do not have time to pick up the chips, your best plan is to lean over the table, surrounding them with your arms. I was forced to do this one evening in a tavern where the space was limited, and I almost wound up as a statistical item. One of the two goons throwing punches at each other accidentally clobbered another player who, like myself, had remained seated. He bounced up quickly with the intention of getting out of the way, but the character who hit him thought he was being ganged, and belted him again—this time on purpose. That did it. The guy went berserk. Knocking the neck off a beer bottle he made for his assailant, who meanwhile had abandoned the other fight and took to the tall timber. He passed right behind my chair with his pursuer jabbing at him with the jagged, razor-sharp bottle neck. I flattened myself on the table and stopped breathing, but even at that the back of my shirt collar was sheared off. There were no casualties because somebody happily thought of fending off the bottle-wielder with a chair, like a lion tamer, until he cooled out.

The business of risking life and limb playing poker does not come up too often, but every now and then you can find yourself in a tough spot. I have always been able to talk or bluff my way out, but sometimes the best thing you can have going for you is a nice hunk of good luck. A hustler I knew, whose specialty was soft games off the beaten path, was playing stud in an outlying neighborhood barroom once and thoughtlessly checked a cinch when the cards were out to one of those iron-hat characters, a dragline operator or something. This happened to be a very unethical thing in this company, and when the pigeon reached across the table for the hustler, nobody interfered. To make matters worse, although built like a heavyweight prospect, the offended

114

party came out with a knife about as long as a bayonet. The hustler figured his number was up because he not only was hemmed in, being seated against the wall, but had an infection on both heels and could not even walk, let alone run, without severe pain. At this critical moment the boss of the joint walked in and broke it up by buying everybody a drink.

Barroom fights usually end when somebody gets knocked cold or if the law happens to blunder in. They are seldom stopped. The opposite is largely true of fights in the public-club and tavern poker games. The House steps in pretty quickly, even if it is a good show. It is bad for business.

50
Camels and Gnats

I once worked for a big organization in the financial colossus class, but that did not stop us from losing our lease in a modern and conveniently located skyscraper at a time when there was a pretty serious shortage of office space. Everybody seemed puzzled as to how it happened, but the reason was quite simple. The top brass handled such matters directly. In spite of repeated notifications from the owner, nobody ever got around to renewing the lease.

With the sheriff breathing down our neck we had to do something in a hurry. We wound up in a musty old trap of a building that had been patched and shined up for use at fancy prices by us and other suckers who also had to take what they could get.

Since the crime was theirs, the top brass could only find comfort in the fact that at least there were floors, walls, and a roof. They laughed off such trifling inconveniences as the world's worst elevator service, a heating-cooling system frequently out of order, and cramped and badly arranged space due to crazy offsets and misplaced columns. However, even they had their limits, and they finally threatened a lawsuit because there was nothing better than paper towels in the dressing rooms.

This sort of thing is known as swallowing a camel and gagging on a gnat or, less elegantly, smiling when you get kicked in the teeth and getting hot under the collar if slapped on the wrist. You hear about such things every day, involving not only individual people but even nations. If one country muscles a piece of another's territory and knocks off a few civilians in the process, you can look for an exchange of notes and maybe even a conference at the diplomatic level; but if the offended country's national pride is wounded because maybe the ambassador did not get the seat he expected at some state dinner, chances are he will start screaming about plots and discrimination, and a big enough stink otherwise will be made to start a war.

Many poker players who do not seem to get excited about important things, such as giving themselves little or no chance to win, often holler copper for no good reason at all. Sometimes you cannot even figure out what inspired the beef, especially when the issue is insignificant, which usually is the case. In a sloppy game one evening a belligerent oaf (who took no notice if somebody passed or called out of turn or otherwise disregarded rules in any way that could have affected the results) threatened to turn the table over because the dealer accidentally flashed a player's hole card and naturally dealt the second card down—a routine procedure. The complainant's argument was that the hole card had not been sufficiently exposed to justify a substitute, and, as it happened to be a small card, he contended that it gave the player an advantage.

Some clubroom operators get top rating in the camel and gnat department. Among other things, they will stand for a con routine from some fast-talking floater a lot quicker than they will go for a modest request from some local producer whom they do not have to worry about. They remind me of city editors I have worked for who would fall all over themselves hiring some guy they had never seen before simply because he walked in and proclaimed that he was good—and pay him more than the tried and true hands.

51
All Is Fair

Poker is about the nearest thing there is to total war. Accordingly, the rules should be observed as is the custom when civilized countries square off against each other. There also should be an absence of niceties and concessions that so frequently are present in some games, especially the sissy games.

Players who act out of turn, fail to put the correct amount of chips in the pot, reveal their hole card when not in the pot, and who otherwise foul up the proceedings not only cause confusion that detracts from the enjoyment of the game but may, and frequently do, affect the result. Since there is no second primary, if you get a hand trimmed because of some player's miscue or indifference you have no recourse as far as the game is concerned. What you do otherwise is your own business, but if discretion does not put the wraps on you there is still a law against mayhem.

One of the toughest rules to get across to certain players is that each player must protect his own hand. If your cards are somehow snafued so that you have an incorrect number, no matter how it happened you are automatically out of action, and no amount of screaming or pleading can change this. A winning hand was neatly slaughtered in a big pot in a public-club game one hot and sticky July afternoon by, of all people, the House dealer. The dealer was working with sleeves rolled up and his arms were moist from perspiration. The player with the top hand was in the last seat on the dealer's right. The latter leaned momentarily on the table to retrieve some discards and accidentally put his under right forearm on top of one of the cards in front of the player. The card clung to it and was dropped into the discard along with the others—a neat crane lift job. The player did not notice it because his back was turned temporarily while fumbling with his drink on a small table behind his chair. When the action was resumed the shortage was discovered, but by this time it was too late. The player not only could not win the pot, but also lost whatever chips he had wagered. I learned later from one of the other players how the mishap occurred. He claimed he was too fascinated to interfere, which I believed because he was in the pot with the next best hand and wound up winning it.

I was high with an ace in a pot once and had nothing else but three small cards including the hole card. There had been little betting, but before the last card fell a dumb-looking pigeon took the lead when I checked. He had a seven, eight, and nine in sight so I figured he probably was drawing to a straight. He caught a bad card and so did I, but I was still high with the ace. I checked the bet and he threw his hand away. I figured that he missed his straight and had decided not to attempt a bluff, so I reached for the pot. He then started an argument, saying that he thought I had said "take it" instead of "check it." He said he had two sevens. His hand was a corpse, but we dug into the discard at my request, and sure enough he did have two sevens. I let him have the pot because I was convinced that he had made an honest mistake. Of course I legally was the winner, but it was too good a chance to make a grandstand gesture at slight cost, so the ham in me prevailed.

While not actually playing friendly or brother-in-law poker, certain players who often play in the same game may have an implied understanding when they wind up head-to-head. The top hand in sight is always supposed to make an honest representation. This usually works out all right, but every now and then the temptation to bluff is hard to resist. This probably results in a standoff, because there is enough larceny in everybody to balance out this kind of situation.

If all poker players would learn that sticking to the rules and regulations and avoiding entangling alliances, even if only implied, are in their interest rather than otherwise, poker may one of these days reach the level of good, clean warfare.

52
Approach with Caution

I played poker for some years with a tough old hustler who would always say, if you lost the first pot you were in, "The vicissitudes of the game are that you should get hooked right away and then play all night to get even."

I have no idea where the ignorant old goat got hold of such a big word, but he was right on the ball as far as logic is concerned. He was simply trying to say that the smart thing to do when you start playing is to strain yourself to keep from losing until you know the score, after which you can start concentrating on trying to win.

In most boxing matches, the fighters spar cautiously for a couple of rounds while feeling each other out. The same is true of football. Fancy maneuvering and angles usually are reserved for later on when more is known of the opponent's strength and tactics.

Conditions in a poker game when you commence playing are

more vague than in boxing and football. Maybe you know every player in the game perfectly and have a solid line on them all, but even this advantage may prove tricky and lure you into a deadfall unless you go through the sparring or feeling-out process. To your specific knowledge of the players (if there are strangers in the game they must be studied closely) should be added two important pieces of information. First, you have to know game tempo, which simply means whether the action is fast or slow. If it is fast, you may scoop in a big pot with one ace; if on the other hand the players have dug in you may find it tough to make two aces win. Putting it another way, the faster the game, the smaller the value of the winning hands (as a rule), and vice versa. The other information you need is current knowledge of the status of each player. If you do not think this is important, try colliding optimistically with a sucker when he is on top, or giving too much respect to the average tough player in bad luck.

Aside from the normal annoyance of getting hooked immediately, which of course cannot always be avoided no matter what you do, the situation is cheerless whether the game is fast or slow. It is bad in a slow game because you frequently fail to get action with good hands, but it can be equally bad or even worse in a fast game if you get a couple of hands knocked off after a poor start. By that time you have had so much action that you are snowed under, and the best you can expect, barring a miracle, is some salvage.

So when you sit in, get your best grip on yourself until you know where you are, unless you are the kind of character who bets hunches instead of form.

120

53
Some Like It Hot

Almost any poker player will tell you that no-limit stud poker is a much tougher game than limit.

It is a rough deal to have somebody bet a chunk at you when you think you have the best hand but could be wrong, and it is also a king-size strain waiting for your opponent to act when you send in your stack on a bluff. Even if all your chips are in the pot with the best hand before the cards are out, you can lose a couple of ounces waiting for the last turn or two to see if your hand will stand up.

In limit poker there is an absence of these tense situations except on rare occasions when an unusually big pot is built up, but the bluffing element is minimized. If you are in there with the worst you are straining to help, and if you have the best you are sweating it out hoping for the cards to break even.

Some poker players confuse the ruggedness of no-limit poker with skill and come up with the conviction that it takes nothing but brains to be a good no-limit player, and at the same time they figure that limit poker is largely a sissy game. In reaching this conclusion they are probably awed by the sudden death or sudden success features of no-limit, and also by the fact that no-limit is the game of the colorful high-stake players.

There are three basic ways of winning when you play no-limit. Number one is having the top hand. The other two ways are bluffing and catching a bluffer. The former unquestionably entails a real hazard, and the latter (at least the majority of times) is simply putting yourself to the guess.

In playing limit poker you are obliged to give consideration to percentages. Your big problem is to save by playing only in pots when your hand meets the minimum standard you have set. You also must consistently strive to reduce competition by the raise, reraise, and the check and raise. All these things take a bit of doing.

In both limit and no-limit the good players figure to win and the bad players figure to lose. The pigeon, however, has the best of it in no-limit. There is nothing to keep him from getting all his chips in and out-drawing the best hand. And he only has to do it once if he is interested in a quick killing, as most pigeons are.

Maybe the best analogy in relating no-limit and limit poker to other activities would be boxing as we know it and the old bare-knuckle days, when the fights were to a finish, in other words no limit. These fights were rough and there was a finality about them that does not exist under today's system of limiting the number of rounds. A fighter can still get knocked out today, and so can a poker player in a limit game, but the proceedings defer basically to skill.

54
Counterpoise

Batting consistently over .500 in poker would be a lot easier if you could make appropriate allowance in advance for all the screwball happenings that have nothing to do with your skill or even the run of the cards. If the players were automatons you could make reasonably safe calculations, but since they are nothing but people there is no way to figure at what moment they will go into a mental tailspin of some kind that scuttles you.

A poker player's passion for Italian style meatballs and spaghetti cost me one of the biggest pots I ever played in. It was not entirely because the player liked this soul-satisfying dish, but it was due to his being notified at precisely the wrong moment that it was being placed on a small table behind his chair. Just as the waiter tapped him on the shoulder it was his turn to act on his hand. He immediately forgot about the pot and turned around to eat. If he had taken the last card, which undoubtedly he would have done if the spaghetti had not arrived, my hand would have stood up, but as it turned out the player behind him caught a case card and beat me.

I was playing limit stud in New Orleans, in the kind of game you dream about, one Saturday afternoon a couple of days before the Sugar Bowl classic. A visiting rooter for the Eastern team was making the game fast by automatically raising every pot or by betting the limit in the blind when he was high. Everybody was getting his load, but I did not hold a hand for hours and was a pretty good loser. Finally my big chance arrived. I was high with an ace and was backed up. I bet and waited confidently for the raise, but meanwhile the loose player had become interested in an old-fashioned dollar bill somebody sitting near him was exhibiting. He not only failed to raise, but he did not even play. He was so interested in the old shin plaster that he threw his hand away without even looking at his hole card.

The Oscar for this sort of thing goes to a player who was in bad luck all evening but at last was about to win his first big pot. When the final card had fallen he had a cinch, but before he could bet a lady stormed in with a six-shooter looking for her husband, and so many guys dived under the table at one time that it tipped over. It turned out that the lady's husband was not in the game after all. She apologized for the intrusion.

55
Name-calling

If you like to play poker every day, you have to take action at the public-club or tavern games. Consequently, you do not always play with other players known to you but frequently find a sprinkling of strangers. This is the rule rather than the exception in such games when business is good, and it is regarded as a healthy situation. Strangers—drop-ins, as they are called—add up to economic stability because each stranger represents fresh money. Regular players are a valuable asset, too, but rotate their participation as finances permit. When only regulars are coming in, business, as a rule, could stand a shot in the arm.

In playing with strangers you are confronted with an Emily Post situation, because even in the public club and tavern games there is a degree of etiquette to be observed—there is not a total absence of something resembling social amenities. In the course of play it is often necessary to address other players, which is no problem if you know them, but if they are strangers they must be addressed in some other manner. There is a seat number penciled in red or blue on the cloth in front of each player. The primary purpose of this is to fix responsibility for each player's ante (a chip of small value that must be put up before a hand is dealt and which constitutes the stake at the beginning of a pot). So as a matter of convenience a player unknown to you may be designated by this number. For example, if the third seat is occupied by a stranger and you wish to say something to him, it would be protocol to address him as "Number Three."

There is, however, an expansion of stranger designation that is more in keeping with the camaraderie of the game. If there is a House dealer or gamerunner (and there usually is in public-club and tavern games) he frequently will bend if not break the barrier of social restraint by giving a stranger an inoffensive designation that is loosely in keeping with the stranger's physical appearance. So "Number Three" may become "Heavy" or "Red" or "Slim" or "Whitey" or "Curley" or any of countless other designations most in keeping with his outstanding physical characteristic. In the absence of an identifying physical characteristic some other term may be used, such as "Pipe" if he happens to be smoking one, or "Tex" if he is wearing a ten-gallon hat or otherwise could be a Texan or at least a "westerner."

Usually you get to know only a small percentage of players by name or occupation. This goes for regulars as well as strangers. Many of the former become known by their first name or sobriquet, but you may play with them for years without any notion of who they are or what they do. Actually, preserving an incognito is quite a simple matter because nobody cares anyway. You have nothing to worry about if you want to keep it that way, unless the law is advertising for your whereabouts or you get yourself splattered on page one for some reason or other.

56
Fools Rush In

If you wish to be a topflight poker player you must develop a strong right arm (unless you happen to be a southpaw—then it is your left biceps that should claim your attention).

In case you think I am mixed up and have major league pitchers in mind, forget it. It is poker I am talking about. You need all the strength you can muster to throw away cards that look good but that in reality are nothing but booby traps.

Every time I play poker I hear losers moan about their tough luck. Maybe they have started with the best hand in big pots five or six times or even more but invariably have finished second. So they figure they are snakebitten. The truth of the matter nearly always is that they have lost more playing hands that should have been junked than they have in all the pots in which they were outdrawn. Naturally they could not be convinced of this, any more than you could sell a female over seven the idea that trapping a husband is not necessarily the only sport life offers. Actually, the great majority of players are not even aware of the squeeze they put on themselves. The rough session they have when in bad luck is often turned into disaster because they play too many bad hands.

The word *standard* is thrown about pretty loosely and most of us just take it in stride, but it is not to be sneezed at as a yardstick for measuring quality. Almost all reputable business organizations and educational institutions are fussy about establishing and maintaining a high standard, which should impress anybody who does not make it a practice of looking down on money and brains.

So if you want to wind up in the win column most of the time you must set yourself a standard when you play poker, and if your cards do not come up to it they should be ditched promptly, no matter how tempting it is to play. There will be times when you would have won certain pots by lowering your standard, as the fall of the cards will reveal, but these exceptions must be viewed without regret. It is tough enough to finish on top when you give the pigeons only grade-A combinations to peck on.

57
Postman's Creed

I knew an old hustler who used to say that it is pretty risky business for a poker player to get caught out in the sun. I suppose he had in mind the fact that poker players usually are not the outdoor type, and might even wind up bedridden if exposed to a mild tan.

Yet, on the other hand, poker players are notorious for their disregard of hardships of any kind that might interfere with their playing. They will come out in the toughest kind of weather, calmly disregarding storms, floods, snow or sleet, high temperature or low, if at the end of the trek they wind up seated behind a stack of chips. Even adverse conditions at the club or tavern or wherever the game happens to be do not cause too much concern. They may curse and swear and rave if the airconditioning conks out in July and the sweat blinds them, or huddle shivering in their overcoats on a blustery winter night if the heating system fails, but, nevertheless, they do not budge for such reasons, taking refuge only in vocal if not necessarily refined resentment.

Many poker players are nothing but addicts. They will show up on Christmas or New Year's Eve or Labor Day as regularly as on any other day. I have played in clubs in New Orleans on Mardi Gras Day when the streets were jammed with revelers and when the Rex and other parades were passing, bands playing, and trim majorettes doing their stuff, and rarely would more than a couple of players leave their seats to see the biggest free show in the world although they had to walk no farther than the front door. The same is true of the television fights. Few players bother to watch them, even if a championship is at stake. Some players act as if they are trying to set speed records on a round trip to the men's room for fear they might miss a hand.

You can give out some blue ribbons—not too many—if the counterinterest has some religious significance. Some players to whom Good Friday has a special meaning will leave the game long enough to attend services at the nearest church of their faith and also may fulfill their Sunday or other holy day obligations. Players of the Jewish faith rarely play the evening before Yom Kippur, the Day of Atonement, but they may sneak in for an hour or two on Yom Kippur itself, because by this time they have made a couple of appearances at the Temple and have publicly established their devoutness. They pursue a related course on Rosh Hashanah, the beginning of the Jewish New Year and a day for meditation, but while they may show at the Temple as a matter of policy, they do most of their meditating in the poker game.

58
No Amateur Athletic Union

In many areas of athletic competition professionals and amateurs may have an equally high rating. This is especially true of golf, where the professionals and amateurs sometimes face each other in tournaments. It also is well known that the amateur tennis champion, immediately after forsaking the rugged activity that rewards only with expense accounts and loving cups, may tangle successfully with the top professional.

The fact that a golfer or tennis star or bridge expert is a professional is no guarantee that he is better than a simon-pure who plays for kicks and has other means of support. It often happens that the amateur triumphs; in fact, some of the stellar performers in more than one highly professionalized sport have been satisfied with medals and trophies. Baseball probably is the outstanding sport wherein this is not true, because everybody knows that all the renowned baseball players are major leaguers who do not seem to be embarrassed by the publicity they get annually arguing with their club for more dough.

As far as poker is concerned it is not too easy to make clear distinctions between those who are professionals and those who are not. Loosely, if a regular player devotes his attention to activities other than work, such as the ponies, but also plays poker because he figures he can win at it, he is a hustler and could be considered a professional. Among people of this kind, however, you will not often find those who play poker exclusively, and even those who do frequently have something else going for them—such as a pension check.

As a class, poker players who could be considered professionals unquestionably surpass those who are not. If for no other reason the former have experience and desire—born of necessity. However, when you take the top players into consideration, it is largely a matter of the individual. The professional usually has the advantage of time and freedom from other obligations. The amateur figures to have a better understanding of the players, because he comes into contact with more different kinds of people, and also usually has educational advantages. The amateur also figures to be more sound financially—a great asset to winning play—because he ordinarily does not have the highs and lows of prosperity experienced by the professional, due to the latter's nonpoker speculations.

One of the greatest misconceptions about poker is the fear some players have of House men. Unless the game is crooked, and nearly all are not, shills are used only to start a game or hold one together. A shill who can break even on an average figures to get a bonus. Shills and other House men who play for themselves when off duty are notoriously bad players. One of the best producers I ever knew managed a club where two or three games were almost always in progress. He signed so many tabs against his salary that he wound up with a bad case of writer's cramp.

59
In Your Sights

All the great fighters had it, from Tom Cribb up through such champions as John L. Sullivan and Jack Dempsey, and no doubt it exists in some of those around today who are now or will become standouts. It also is a component of conquerors, whose triumphs in war or peace very probably could not have been achieved without it. You can use any kind of language you like, but neither subtleties nor rhetorical flourishes can change the basic fact that this greatest of assets to success is simply the killer instinct.

If you have your opponent at a disadvantage and fail to tear in and destroy him, you are lacking in the primitive ferocity that pays such big dividends. Cynics will assure you that you not only may never get another opportunity, but also may be setting yourself up for the full treatment at some future time.

You can learn from poker, which teaches so many lessons, that the quality of mercy should not be strained. Unless you profit to the fullest possible extent when calling the shots, you are simply taking the worst of it and at the same time actually helping nobody. It is true that, by pulling your punches when you should be going in for the kill, you might reap some kind of hypocritical gratitude, but the beneficiary of your misguided generosity very likely will secretly despise you.

Sympathy fits in pretty well in certain spots, but it is about as out of place in a poker game as a skunk in the kitchen. If you take it easy against a player in bad luck you may only be giving some-

131

body else an opportunity to win the chips that should have been yours. You also are not doing the unlucky player any good because the only way he can recoup is to get legitimate action, which you are denying him by your phony kindness. Furthermore, you are putting him in the uncomfortable position of being grateful—for nothing. When a player gives me the sympathy routine I try to express my appreciation by checking a cinch into him at the first opportunity—or otherwise knocking his brains out.

60
They Remember You

Among the many aspects that add up to the fascination of poker is the challenge it offers to excel on your own, because you are in there with nobody but opponents. Discounting luck, which gives you a standoff over the years anyway, you take or distribute lumps in direct ratio to your playing ability.

If the foregoing is correct it may account for the lasting impressions created in the minds of certain players. You may play the game objectively, giving little thought to the other players as individuals (except only as their habits and personality traits may affect their play), but some put it on a more personal basis. They are inclined to associate their poker experiences, especially the unpleasant ones, with those who figured in them.

Elephants are credited with having a remarkable memory, particularly if they have it in for somebody who mistreated them, and camels also have been given honorable mention in this department, to say nothing of the American Indian. However, with all due respect to these classic grudge-bearers, I give the palm to poker players who are able to retain the details of some hand that was played in the distant past in which you were the villain, but which you probably forgot in ten minutes.

One day a visiting stranger in a public game in New Orleans beat me out of a small pot. He was well dressed and gentlemanly appearing, about middle age, and he remarked, as he gathered in the chips, that it was a happy occasion for him because it was the first time he ever won a pot off me. This was puzzling because I did not recall ever having played with him before. When I told him this he promptly gave me the particulars of a couple of pots he lost to me, including the hands we each held, how much was in the pots, and how the play developed in both instances. I would have assumed that we had played recently, maybe the day previously, and that he had changed his appearance by shaving his mustache or something, but he informed me in response to my question that he only arrived in town that morning after an absence of nearly five years.

Sometimes you meet people in other settings and they not only will astonish you by recalling the occasions they played poker with you, but will have at their fingertips the full and complete stories of the sneaky tactics you employed to rack them up. Good breeding requires that you pretend to remember them, besides which, as a balm to their possible ill will, you hasten to assure them that they unfortunately caught you on what undoubtedly must have been one of your rare, exceptionally good days.

61
Look Her Squarely in the Eye

I knew a poker player whose wife was convinced that he was an ardent fisherman. As far as she was concerned he went fishing almost every weekend or holiday and usually brought back some fish, which he either sent to the market for or arranged for some legitimate fisherman to bring him. For greater authenticity—as he believed in leaving nothing to chance—he would stand in the sun just long enough to acquire a bit of outdoor seasoning, because otherwise his wife might begin to suspect that his fishing trips never got any further than the poker game.

If the poker player's wife had known that he was absent from home so frequently to play poker, the chances are a showdown would have occurred long since, but fishing—that was different. His absence for the salutary purpose of fishing was okay, because all he could do was spend whatever the trip cost and perhaps lose his life, as fishermen occasionally fall overboard and drown. But poker, emphatically no! It naturally is not too difficult to understand the wife's concern for the family bankroll, but I believe the reason is a bit deeper than that. Although many women play poker it almost always is not the true masculine brand, so when their husbands' eyes sparkle at the prospect of a real poker game the wives instinctively arch their backs. Could be there is a little jealousy mixed up in it, like anything else they feel they are completely out of.

The married poker player who has to dream up some excuse

134

to get to the game becomes a master of originality. Obviously he cannot continue to use the pleas of working overtime or sitting up with a sick friend. So he has to meet an important customer at the airport, spring somebody who has been arrested for arguing with a traffic cop, help set up a meeting of a civic organization committee, attend a political rally or find himself involved in something else that can get him out of the house for several hours with no questions asked.

Many poker players who got to the game the hard way before free television doings, took advantage of night sports activities. Boxing had long been a favorite dodge, abetted during recent years by night baseball and football. Nearly all poker players interested in domestic tranquillity were careful to keep themselves posted on the time such events ended, especially fights, which were liable to wind up in a quick knockout. Some wives, however, got such information themselves by telephoning the newspapers. One metropolitan sports editor, pretending to be writing a funny editorial on the subject, in reality tipped off all husbands in the community, poker players or otherwise.

The palm for inventiveness goes to the poker player to whom getting out was extremely tough. He simply found it necessary to attend a wake several times a month. His wife never suspected, because his business and fraternal activities brought him into contact with a great many people, but he did hear her tell somebody once how sad it was that her husband's friends were dying like flies.

62
Long Green

A wise Congress passed a law not too long ago protecting stock speculators with short bankrolls from themselves. Formerly, if you wished, you could buy stock by depositing a small percentage of the market value, which was known as buying on margin. If the stock held or went up, well and good; but if it hit the skids you not only took a beating by the loss of most if not all of your investment, you had no chance to recoup or make a profit if the stock subsequently came to life. So now it is illegal to buy less than a substantial interest when you dabble in the market, resulting at least theoretically in fewer burned fingers.

No matter what the activity, whether it is operating a peanut stand or starting a war, your chances of success dwindle if you have a skimpy wad. In poker the handicap more often than not is fatal. Players suffering with the shorts are under constant pressure and take so much the worst of it otherwise that, even if they are experienced, they figure to lose.

The best weapon of the no-limit poker player is money—gobs of it. It is pretty easy to bluff the short-money player who has only five or ten percent of his chips in action and you bet him the rest. He not only has to consider the possibility that you are not bluffing, but also the danger of having the best hand outdrawn. You also have it on him if he is lucky enough to double his chips against you once or more often. You can try again and again and the first time you win he is knocked out. You leave him with two alternatives: to quit while he is ahead or keep a tight grip on his horseshoe.

Some suckers actually penalize themselves with the short-money routine. They will buy eight or ten times in small amounts and suffer all the disadvantages of the short-money player. Very often they lose with good hands because they cannot bet enough (and this happens in limit as well as no-limit), or they do not win what they should because frequently they have interest only in a portion of the pot, because all their money is in and they are sighting. These chumps will argue that their system works both ways, that by having less they lose less when beaten. From their viewpoint this position often could be logical, because most of them are not in there to win, but to last.

Moral: If you are going to set off some dynamite, do not fool around with a short fuse.

63
Partisans

Most of us seem to have developed the cute but usually subconscious habit of relating ourselves to situations in which we are not direct participants but which affect our emotions. This sort of thing even goes so far, according to one authority, that we recognize and pay tribute to genius because in genius we see something of ourselves—a much better article, beyond doubt—but still us. So the next time you are watching a boxer on television using his chin to block his opponent's punches, and pull for the underdog to turn the tide by connecting with a lucky haymaker, in a way you are rooting for yourself.

137

If you boil it down, probably one of the best things we do anyway is take sides. Unless we are personally involved (for example, if we have a chunk riding on the favorite in a football game), we are inclined to cheer for the weaker side. We charge this to our sportsmanship or sense of fair play, whether the situation involves athletic competition, politics, the office, or a bit of mayhem perpetrated on her husband by an unjustly suspicious wife.

Every time you play poker situations arise that find you taking sides—covertly as a rule, except when your satisfied expression, if the result is what you wished, speaks more eloquently than mere words. The big winners and heels you pull against as a matter of form. You also nearly always pull against players anywhere near your own class. Interest prompts this for obvious reasons, not the least being the fact that getting knocked off may tend to soften them up.

Unless entirely devoid of human feelings, your heart goes out in full sympathy to the hapless pigeon continually braving one-sided odds. Time and again you would like to step in and halt the proceedings by making the pigeon understand that once more he is knee-deep in bear traps, but all you can do is hope that somehow the sheep will get an unexpected break and wind up killing the butcher.

Witnessing the plucking of a pigeon is a sad and painful experience, because every time you are only watching it, there is that much less for you to get your hooks into.

64
Liquid Ire

One of the toughest rules of just about all public-club and tavern poker games prohibits anybody from putting his drink on the table. Lushes are quickly pounced on, but the rule applies to all. The standard price is eight-to-five that the drink will be tipped over if it is allowed to remain. The only reason there is not plenty of action on this proposition is the fact the House will not stand for it. Nobody cares too much if a player gets it in his lap, but there is nothing messier or more inconvenient in a poker game than a wet tablecloth.

Sudden and unexpected contact with liquid of any kind can be disconcerting—even mildly shocking. That is why nobody has improved on the time-honored method of breaking up a dogfight by dousing the mutts with water. It also has been pretty well established that a good stream from a fire hose can often do more to disperse an unruly mob than the threat of machine guns.

I went to a football game at the Sugar Bowl stadium once with a plunger who had a big chunk riding on the result. We were anxious to arrive on time and had given ourselves a fair margin to make it for the kickoff but found the ramps unusually congested due to some gate-crashing. Our portal was so jammed when we reached it that we could only inch forward, consequently the game was under way long before we glimpsed the playing field. We elbowed through at last, but the final obstacle was a silly-looking young dame standing squarely in front of us. Her arms were

139

spread out because in each hand she held a highball in a king-size paper cup. My friend threw a gentle block on her, causing some of the stuff to spill. She turned to glare, a bit unamicably. Instead of apologizing while continuing to apply pressure to dislodge her, my friend thoughtlessly made an innocent observation about jerks, especially female ones, who come to football games only to drink and annoy other people. His remark seemed to crush the little lady. She was so ashamed that she promptly got rid of the high-balls, pouring one down my friend's collar and aiming the other at his head, where she scored a bull's-eye. And my friend? He was magnificent. He did not even look back. He hesitated only long enough to whisper to a startled woman nearby, who was splashed a bit, that she should smack the little gal, since it was no chore for a gentleman. Fortunately, the weather was mild, so my friend came out of it needing only a dry-cleaning job.

The business of tossing a drink in somebody's face to produce a dramatic reaction is a standard theatrical gimmick. It clicks best when the victim is undeserving of the insult but, because of circumstances, must submit without retaliation. The audience, in the know, enjoys suffering with the gallant martyr.

The best poker game use I have ever noted of a drink that did not go down the hatch was when an inoffensive little man, needled for a couple of hours by a flannelmouth, designed and executed his own peculiar revenge. He ordered a small bottle of beer just before cashing in his chips and, simulating obsequious friendship for the ribber, told him he had a hot horse going in the first heat at Hialeah the following day. As he leaned over to whisper the details he calmly poured the beer into the big heel's coat pocket and was long gone before the soggy cigarettes and the general clamminess of the garment were discovered.

65
Ananias Was a Piker

Some years back a lush in whom I was interested and wanted to help said that he had decided to climb on the water wagon. He thought he should do it in style, so at his request I accompanied him to a church rectory where he could sign the pledge. Matters progressed smoothly enough until the clergyman asked him for how long he wanted to take the pledge, at which point the lush looked a bit pained and replied that he usually took it for life.

Many poker players, as a matter of routine, quit the game for good at regular intervals. They do not sign a pledge, but some go in for dramatic effect in announcing their retirement, especially right after getting a big hand knocked off. Now and then a couple of characters quit together for life and work out a forfeit deal which requires the one who weakens first to pay the other a stipulated amount. I have never known such an arrangement to wind up in anything but a standoff because the two finally get tired of playing hide-and-seek with each other and weaken simultaneously.

The unreliability of statements made in solemn sincerity by poker players is by no means confined to their announced intention to give up the game. A poker player rarely tells the truth while a hand is being played, hence the advice that you should never believe a poker player did not exactly get to be standard for frivolous reasons. If a stud hand has three cards of the same suit in sight before the last card falls and if the player pulls for a flush, figure him for a pair, and vice versa. If a player tells you he has got you, it is usually wise to call him; if he says you have got him, chances are you will make money in the long run by passing. No matter what may be said about the hand during the action, figure on the opposite. The best way to cross up your opponents, if you must play the game with your mouth, is to tell them the truth.

Lawyers who tee off on each other in court and apparently are prevented from committing assault only by tough threats from the bench, as likely as not may be found amicably sharing the same table during the recess for lunch. The courtroom scene was only part of the show—possibly produced by the excitement of the legal conflict but more probably to impress their respective clients.

The same sort of thing happens quite often in poker games during the heat of the action. If you figure that you will see a swell free fight almost any second if two players needle each other throughout the playing of the hand, you will probably be doomed to disappointment, because the belligerents rarely get beyond the talking stage. With the end of the action is the end of the interest, especially because the winner now has all the satisfaction he wants, and it takes two to start or continue an argument.

Whatever a poker player may say while he is playing poker, copper it; but if you must be trusting, give yourself a break: do not take it with a grain of salt, make it a dose.

66
Shock Absorber

Admirers of the late Rocky Marciano, who retired undefeated as heavyweight champ, mostly remember him for his ability to knock his opponents bow-legged. He did not stop them all, but the ones who stayed on their feet were belted around so good that Marciano never failed to get the duke if the fight went the limit, which was the reason he wound up with forty-nine wins, zero losses.

Rocky could dish it out all right, but he could also take it, which maybe was the real reason he got to be champion in the first place. No matter how hard a fighter can hit, he figures to stop some wallops with his chin, so unless he can weather a few storms along the way he will not get the chance to show how good he is at dishing it out. The same is true of other champions, no matter what their field. Washington was on the canvas at Valley Forge but beat the count, and Napoleon took his lumps at Abukir and a couple of other places before and after he got to be emperor. When he blew the decision at Waterloo he was only a has-been trying to make a comeback.

The business of absorbing punishment is a standout requirement of successful poker playing. Not running out of money is, of course, elemental, but you also cannot run out of control—which a series of thumpings can produce—unless you have the ability to take it going for you.

You are never in a position to judge a poker player until you see him losing. A player can look so good when he is getting the breaks that you can easily come up with the wrong line on him, so it is a mistake to tab him for keeps until you see how he reacts to a few shellackings.

Race horse players will tell you that some horses are terrific if they manage to jump out on top and get to the wire unchallenged. They may even set a new track record. However, if another horse gets close enough to breathe on them, these same horses are likely to quit cold. They just do not have it in them to keep trying when the going gets tough, or in other words they cannot take it.

Keeping a strangle-hold on yourself when bucking a bad losing streak is the acid test of the poker player. You are not only put to the strain of avoiding the sucker route when you are getting the best hand knocked off about ninety-eight percent of the time, but you also have to worry about staying healthy in case you let some ape needle you into coming up with tough wisecracks.

67
More on Checking Cinches

My views on checking a cinch in stud poker are well known, so there is no need at this time to expound repetitiously on the position I have already taken. I suppose that I am prompted to bring up the subject more than any other poker "issue," because I am ever-lastingly amazed at those players—and there are many of them—who believe that the practice not only is reprehensible, sneaky, and contemptible, but also quite detestable.

The speedballs of the big no-limit games are unenthusiastic about cinch checking, particularly if it is done when the cards are out, which creates a deadfall, because there is no chance to draw out. (It will be noted that I have used the word *cinch* in the context of check and raise, but it is my position that a cinch is the best hand during any of the four betting intervals in stud poker.) A fast player in high-stakes games may, of course, check a cinch himself if he thinks his opponent will bet. However, he seems to prefer, in most cases, the weapons of bluff and psychology.

Now, human nature being what it is, the other players in the big games do not like to see the speedballs slowed down, which can happen if there is a tough tightwad at the table waiting patiently for the chance to brain the unwary. And I am with those other players, too—up to a point. The point is that I join them only insofar as I am, myself, excepted. The fact is, I would not play if deprived of one of my best moves, actually my most productive play. It would be the same as if a football quarterback were hampered by a regulation *requiring* him to pass when he backs up or scrambles, looking for a receiver; or requiring him to hand the ball to his fullback or other ball carrier, or keep it himself if he remains close to the line of scrimmage after he gets the ball from his center. A parallel situation would exist in poker if a player holding top hand could not check, and raise, if the opportunity is afforded in the same betting interval.

Incidentally, in just about all poker games, the checking of a cinch (as I have mentioned in other works when handling this topic expansively) may be accomplished, in effect, by the sneaky maneuver of betting a chip of ante value instead of checking, hoping that some other player will interpret the smallness of the bet as weakness of the hand. Strangely enough, this may be done without censure even from the intellectual Goliaths who condemn the unspeakable check and raise. I could be asked why I do not just bet an ante chip instead of checking when I have a cinch. A fair question. I have tried it, but for some unaccountable reason it seems to suggest the possibility of a trap and definitely does not work as well as the brutal *checking* of a cinch.

There is a premium that I and other cinch checkers earn that I have not so far mentioned. When you are known to make a habit of checking cinches, and your hand in sight looks formidable, you get quite a number of free cards during the course of an evening's play, because your opponents, as a rule, are leery of betting into you.

68
They Eat It with a Spoon

I read some place once that the best way to get an important person obligated to you is to let him do you a favor.

The wise guy who came up with that one must have figured that if such a person gives you a lift he takes you on as a personal responsibility, and maybe his pride is dented if you stumble, so he has to pick you up again. Of course the truth could be that he did you the favor in the first place to set you up for something he had in mind later on and kept the thing going to protect his investment.

This flyer into trying to dope out one of the angles of what is called human nature leads to more of the same, such as what a cinch it is to give almost anybody the business if you know where to find the soft spot in his head. You can refine the oil or dish it up crude, it is all the same as long as you keep pouring.

Almost any poker player will go for a smooth con routine now and then that will cost him some chips, but you have a pretty good chance of knocking yourself out at it as a steady diet. Nearly all players, even pigeons, figure that any kind of patter during the action is nothing but a gimmick to set them up for the kill.

Poker players can be had, though, if you want to swing them over to your side for some reason or other, provided that they do not get hip to your pitch. I wormed my way into a dream game that produced a steady supply of fat pigeons some time back, but I was never sure that the red carpet would not be jerked from

146

under me at any moment. In spite of the fact that I pulled my punches and acted plenty dumb, I never had more than half a foot in the door. The main stumbling block was an ignorant old goat who was the political bigwig of the precinct, a pretty fair player who took a dim view of my intrusion into his private preserves. I threw all kinds of curves at him to soften him up but could not score, until finally I tried repeating one of his corny wisecracks and giving him the credit line. From that moment I was a charter member. The old bum liked to be quoted.

As I said, the trick is to find the soft spot in the victim's head and ooze in the malarky as if you are leveling, but sometimes you can overdo it. I worked a boy-scout routine in a game one night, telling an outstanding heel, who was nothing but an animated cadaver and who probably had at least a couple of serious ailments, that I had never seen him looking so healthy and was glad he was taking such good care of himself. He picked it up from there and in no time at all was a well man again.

69
If You Have Nose Trouble, See a Specialist

Helping a feeble old lady cross a busy intersection would seem to be a chivalrous act, and ordinarily it is. However, it could happen that the old lady does not want to be helped, and you might wind up being menaced by an umbrella, especially if she figured that you were using a dodge to snatch her purse.

People who need assistance are not always in the market for the helping hand. If they do not get the idea that you are simply a meddler, they may conclude that you have an interest of some kind that may cost them something. So you should be pretty certain in advance that your kindly offices are desired before you go into your Good Samaritan act. I have heard more than once of a chivalrous citizen getting worked over by both parties for interfering with a wife-clobbering husband.

There are certain poker players—every game has them—who may be counted on to jeopardize their rights because they are guilty of foolish indiscretions. No matter how many years they may have played poker (which would seem to make adherence to routine procedures instinctive), they will commit some flagrant error every now and then that will nullify or at least jeopardize a winning hand. Trying to protect people like this is a hazard, because at the moment it may seem to them that you are only being an obnoxious kibitzer and would do better minding your own business.

Some players hate to show a losing hand after the final call. Theoretically, all hands should be shown, but frequently the loser throws his hand into the discard. It sometimes happens that the winning hand is overlooked. The player may have been concentrating on making a pair and made a straight or a flush without noticing it; or he may have misread his hole card and actually had a pair and did not realize it.

There is another fairly common situation that is even goofier. If a player is bluffing and gets called he may say, "That's good," before his opponent exposes his hole card. The latter may then fold his hand without further ado and throw it into the discard without showing the hole card. When this happens the original bettor (the bluffer), whose hand is still alive, is in position to claim the pot. The only way, usually, you can stop the player with the winning hand from cutting his own throat is to yell sharply at him or physically prevent him from fouling his hand—in either case risking his resentment. You also do not make your-

148

self too popular with the loser, who perhaps is the kind of character who does not mind winning a pot on a technicality.

There is a reverse action, also. Sometimes players expose the hole card too quickly before the betting is completed. This may cost only another call, but it also could—and sometimes does— cost the pot, because some player still to act (thinking he is beaten until he happily sees the other hand) takes over.

Protecting a mentally feeble player from himself is a fine and praiseworthy act—particularly if you keep in mind the fact that he later may lose to you the chips you keep him from throwing away.

70
They Give Ice to Eskimos

The tightwad poker player is a reasonable facsimile of his blood brother who may be encountered anywhere else. Generally he is narrow, suspicious, and mean but on occasion can be a boon companion—if there are free doings.

The run-of-the-mill tightwad, poker player or not, keeps the whip on himself relentlessly. No matter what he does he relates it to money. If he dreams on Christmas Eve, instead of sugarplums his visions are likely to be wholesale prices, discounts, and special rates. When he gives something away he expects more commercials than a television spectacular.

I played poker for years with an outstanding tightwad who was alone in the world and did nothing but add to his relatively substantial hoard, which he entrusted only to such institutions as postal savings and homesteads. He knew almost to the penny how much he would spend daily and was not above saving a nickel or a dime by such means as carrying his own tray in a cafeteria. We lived in the same neighborhood, a long haul from the game, and I frequently drove him home. I did not have my car one night and figured that this was a chance for him to reciprocate. I was not optimistic enough to think he would offer to pay the full taxi fare, so I propositioned him on a fifty-fifty basis. Although the weather was cold and disagreeable and it was two o'clock in the morning, he said he would wait for the two-thirty bus, which took him within three blocks of his house, entailing a lonely and dangerous walk down a tree-lined street. He made it in spite of the fact that I was pulling hard for a stickup.

A tight poker player does not give himself much of a chance. He is altogether different than a tough player, who has sufficient flexibility to take a legitimate risk. The tight player simply sits there and throws away hand after hand until he gets a 24-karat combination. Consequently he wins few pots, and if he gets a couple of hands knocked off he is almost hopelessly hooked. He takes so little action that the ante and other tariffs melt away most of his chips.

Tight players have a lot in common. If they get off on top they will take almost any kind of profit and quit, but if hooked they are glued to the chair for many a long hour. They make themselves miserable worrying about how much the House takes from the pots, and they often have tough arguments with the porter about the price of a sandwich or some other item. Their conversation usually runs to moans about taxes and the high cost of living.

A tight player of long acquaintance, for whom I was able to do a favor that had nothing to do with poker, offered to give me a confidential rundown on his method of play, which he indicated was intricate. This character was known as the Rock of Gibralter, or simply the Rock. I told him his kindness overwhelmed me but was not necessary, since I had figured out years previously

150

that his abstruse formula consisted entirely of playing nothing but cinches.

Tight players rarely come out ahead by the year. Even if they win more often than they lose—and some do—their winnings per play are small, and when they have a bad session it is usually a killer. They get little action because even the dumbest suckers quickly get wise to them. If reduced to statistics the chances are it would be discovered that ninety-nine out of a hundred tight players are simply tight suckers.

71
Soothing Syrup

Bad winners at poker are much more obnoxious than bad losers.

It is sort of elemental. Bad winners have already made themselves disagreeable by the mere fact of being on top, so their gloating and smart talk simply add to an already annoying situation. On the other hand, bad losers may be grade-A heels whose misery you enjoy, or unwitting comics good for a laugh. It also should be remembered that they have paid for the privilege of a few plain and fancy beefs.

If you boil it down, the bad poker winner is simply in character. He is no doubt a bad winner otherwise. Poker, as it does with the personality traits of nearly all players, brings the full measure of the bad winner's unsavory instincts to the fore. It is largely the same with other characteristics. So if you are a fink or a bully playing poker, it is a pretty safe bet that you are a fink or a bully.

Bad winners in poker games probably amused themselves as kids in innocent and harmless little exercises such as sticking pins through live insects, and it may safely be assumed that not all of such gentle inclinations vanished by the time they started shaving. I used to play draw with a benevolent character who enjoyed telling you how very lucky you were when you held a big hand, such as a flush—if he had just finished knocking it off for you.

Some bad winners like to give you the needle. They will let you think that the pot is yours and then show you the winning duke. For example, if you call a representation of two aces in stud with two kings, one of these fun-loving characters will say, "That's good," and when you reach for the pot will add, "—if you can beat two aces." It is a soothing experience to be on the short end of this gag, especially when you are hooked up to your eyebrows.

Quitting weak games early and unexpectedly is one of the favorite practices of some bad winners. If they would just get up and quit nobody would mind too much, but they like to give out with some baloney like, "I'm going to have a tough day at the office tomorrow and I need my rest," or "I have to pick up the wife at the movies."

Bad winners have a lot in common. Among other things they seem to believe that there is no symphony that matches the sound of their own voice.

72
Anything for a Laugh

One evening when about five or six poker games were going in one of the biggest public clubs in town, somebody struck an old-fashioned kitchen match and it popped like a pistol shot. A minute or so later another popping match did its stuff, and soon after it was strictly Fourth of July. Some fun-loving Rover Boy had mixed up about a hundred popping matches with the big box of honest lucifers on the counter. He and a couple of other nitwits previously had made the round of the tables, dropping them into coat pockets or, when unobserved, laying them conveniently near players. The joint was in an uproar until anything that looked like a kitchen match was confiscated. The winners thought it was a pretty good gag, especially since nobody lost an eye and the heart cases took the explosions in stride.

The cuter the pixie the more trouble he will go to for a laugh. One of the favorite routines is to swipe book matches from near-sighted old gentlemen, ignite the warheads, set out to cool, and then surreptitiously return them apparently intact to the owners. This takes a bit of doing, but when the victims peevishly strike match after match without result it rolls the pranksters in the aisle.

Some characters figure it is good, clean fun to drive House men nuts. In one game the dealer, not quite a brain-truster, kept calling for fresh stacks of ante chips. A wag had persuaded the players to ante up a quarter chip each time, keeping the half-nickel ante chips and the nickel chips out of sight. The gag finally skidded to a halt when the joint ran out of low caliber ammo.

If any comics are in the House and the floor man has a low boiling point, one of the surefire gimmicks is to keep him running back and forth to the cashier's cage by changing the decks, buying chips that are not needed, exchanging big chips for stacks of smaller ones, and vice versa, until he finally tumbles and puts the blast on everybody, which of course provides the payoff giggle.

Lushes get a pretty good working over with such corny items as fake telephone calls and false rumors. Some guys like to be original, and pull such tricks as playfully picking up a gob of chips from a lush when he is not looking. The general idea is to get the lush to start a bum argument with somebody else and then slip the missing chips back, persuading the lush that they were there all the time. Once the joke backfired. The lush did not even notice the difference. Not wishing to subject himself to unnecessary embarrassment, the jokester took the easy way out. He kept the chips.

Some of us who played poker every day in the City Hall pressroom some time back were pretty sharp cookies. Our practical jokes did not go much beyond the hotfoot stage, but we were a riot when it came to original gags in the subtle department. If somebody started panning somebody else who was not present, we would put out the fire with the well-he-always-speaks-nice-about-you routine. Another of our gems ran something like this. If somebody called somebody else a crummy old bum we would defend the accused by remarking that he was not so old. We gave it all up when we began to notice that professional gag men were using our stuff in the movies and elsewhere. We were afraid that the standards would get too high and that some of the professional gagsmiths would lose their job if they ever had to get back on their own.

73
On Quitting

When to quit the poker game is a player decision restricted almost entirely to the public-club, tavern, and other commercial games. It does not figure to be a problem in the private games, as a rule, because starting and quitting times have been established. It may happen, however, that irreconcilable disagreement may cause a player to quit prematurely, and this also may occur if a player inconveniently reaches the limit of his finances.

In the nonprivate games reasons for quitting are indeed varied.

A big winner may wish to get away with his profit. A big loser may quit because he is tapped out, or if not for that reason may decide that his run of bad luck is such that he had better wait for another time. Any number of other reasons also may cause players to retire from the game, the main reason being the time element.

There is a rather wide divergence of opinion on the advisability of quitting if the consideration is not wanting to risk losing chips already won. Incidentally, as most regular players will affirm, there is more pain associated with loss from winnings than with loss from the original investment. Sharp, experienced players usually say that playing time should be extended to the very limit, or even beyond, if you are ahead. Not only may it be assumed that the run of the cards is favorable, but there also figures to be improvement in the winner's play, born of the heady intoxication of confidence. These same individuals are inclined to take an opposite view when things are not going well, particularly if the losing streak includes consistent defeat of good hands. You know you are up against it when you have the best hand to go in stud, help it, and still lose. For example, starting with aces back-to-back and making aces up, and a set of threes or a flush or straight rakes in the chips.

There are still other reasons of a general nature for quitting in the commercial games. A winner may desire to play longer but sometimes will considerately quit the game to make room for some other regular player who may have waited a couple of hours or even longer for a seat. It also may happen that a winner whose judgment dictates quitting will remain in the game an additional period as a friendly gesture to the House, even though well aware that the pace of the game has slowed due to reduced player complement.

74
Suspicion

It is not a bad idea to be on the watchful side when doing business with strangers (and keenly alert if with relatives or friends), but you can overdo it. After all, we should not be as suspicious as the old crud who was helped up from a bad fall in the street, and rewarded the kind stranger by calling the cops and having him arrested as a pickpocket suspect.

People who figure that everybody is trying to give them the business are more likely to get it than those who at least want to see a little smoke before they holler fire. This is not too strange because hardly anybody—even crooks—likes to be distrusted, which of itself could lead to shenanigans if for no other reason than the power of suggestion.

Certain newcomers to poker games give all players the sidelong glance treatment. They do not have to tell you that they think they have stumbled into a den of thieves—their demeanor and actions proclaim it. When they lose a pot they figure that it was a cooler, and if they win they think that the dealer slipped up or that the victory was just a come-on. In further evidence of their slight lack of confidence, they watch every move everybody makes and weigh carefully everything that is said, because they are fearful of signals and other crooked proceedings. As added precautions they change the decks frequently, and carefully scrutinize the backs and edges of the cards for any telltale scratch or blemish.

156

Players who have been chased by a bear almost always are nothing but rank suckers. Their attitude probably is born of the dismal experience of repeated shellackings, which they are unable or unwilling to account for other than by the ego-satisfying conclusion that they were taken.

About the worst thing you can do is assure suspicious newcomers that they are surrounded by honest citizens, because they instantly interpret this as a clever defense mechanism, and you may wind up being the number one suspect. I tried it out one evening on such a doubter who was making insinuating references about the thinness of the plastic deck when it was his turn to deal, by calling his attention to the fact that it figured to feel somewhat smaller to the grip than a standard deck. I was touched by his trust in me as he held up the game to count the cards to prove I was right.

Sometimes suspicious attitudes can become infectious. If you are hooked you are liable to start wondering if maybe there is not a magician or two in the game, and if on top you start hoping you do not hold any big hands on your own deal. It reminds me of the frequent sermons of a kindly and sincere old clergyman, a throwback to the Dark Ages, who constantly harped on the relentless efforts of Lucifer to corrupt and betray trusting souls by persistent and appealing temptations. The good man warned his congregation to maintain eternal vigilance and never failed to emphasize that Lucifer cleverly assumed many forms and guises. Before he finished you usually edged a bit away from the strangers in your pew, and maybe even quit giving the eye to the good-looking gal across the aisle for fear she was only a juicy bait of the Evil One.

157

75
He Shaved Us without Soap

Everybody knows about paper routes and bread routes and milk routes and all kinds of other routes, but I knew a character who had a poker route.

He was especially busy on weekends. From Friday through Sunday he would play in half a dozen or more different games, sometimes three in the same evening. He tried to hit a game at the peak of the action, make a quick killing, and then move on to the next scene of operations.

I played with him for years but knew him only as the Barber. He actually operated a barber shop, but why he wasted his time fooling with haircuts and shaves was a big mystery, because he consistently knocked poker games bow-legged. He was by no means a rough-and-tumble player who would take after you with the worst of it, but if he figured his hand was the best to go, no matter how narrow the margin, he would plow aggressively until a big pot was built up.

The Barber made mathematical percentages look pretty silly. If you had him trapped he would draw out, but if his hand was the best the cards would break even. Naturally, this did not always happen, but it happened so often that you were whipped before you started. If you chanced to have a hand stand up against him or outdrew him you figured you were the beneficiary of a miracle. Even when you beat the stinker you rarely did it with a summertime hand. If he did not catch big cards or make a pair of some kind in sight, he would wind up with a possible straight or flush—always enough to slow you down and keep you worried.

The Barber was a freak because over a period of years his phenomenal good luck never changed. When he had an occasional bad night it would be followed by forty good ones. He played a sharp game and outsmarted pigeons and even fair players right and left, but his luck was so good that it overcame some pretty important basic defects in his play.

Some players thought the Barber fooled around with the deck and came up with too many backed-up big pairs when he dealt. They also claimed that if he did not start with a big pair when dealing, he caught nothing but aces and paints. They were undoubtedly right about the cards he caught when drawing, but that happened just as regularly when he was not dealing. Most of the times that he outdrew me for big pots I was handling the deck myself, a pretty fair safeguard. Whether he dealt or not it was the same story. He either somehow had the percentages working for him in reverse or used mass hypnotism and we just thought he was helping.

One time the Barber stumbled into a tavern game deep in the Bougalee country of Louisiana and, being in form, pretty soon had everybody digging. The other players discussed the situation among themselves in their native Cajun-French and agreed that the only smart thing to do was to give the Barber the business at the first opportunity if they wanted to get their money back. This might have worked if the Barber had not understood every word they had said because, while his long residence in the city made his appearance deceptive, he was a Bougalee himself.

76
Fair for One

It probably is a natural instinct, when you continue getting clobbered at whatever game you are playing, to think of squaring
accounts by taking on your opponents in some other game where
you figure to do better—you think.

Many players in limit-poker games find themselves so situated.
They not only take a dim view of their high percentage of losses,
but also build up a king-size resentment against consistent winners.
In due course the losers arrive at the rather remarkable conclusion
that the fault does not lie with them at all. The answer is quite
simple: the game is all wrong.

The favorite chant of many losers is that they get hands knocked
off because they cannot bet enough, cannot protect a hand. Their
lament implies that by playing with a limit they are at some sort
of personal disadvantage, like being forced to fight with one arm
tied down. You get the idea from that point on that if they ever
lure you into a no-limit game your goose is cooked, because then
the scales will turn automatically in their favor.

While acknowledging that there are some sharp differences in
limit and no-limit poker, bad players who squawk bloody murder
because they are restricted in betting by the limit, as a rule fare
just about the same in the no-limit game—maybe worse in one
sense, because usually they do not last as long. What they overlook
is the fact that the no-limit privileges are not restricted to them but

are the same for all players. Some real bad players who figure to go broke in any game may have a little the best of it in no-limit, because they will take all kinds of ridiculous chances and may make a killing if they get lucky.

A good limit player is almost always a good no-limit player, but the reverse of this is not necessarily true. Some good no-limit players find themselves outclassed playing with a limit, because they have developed certain techniques that are of little value in playing limit. For example, if they clock a representation of two jacks accurately and set out to pair a queen, some other player may be doing the same thing with a king or an ace, unlikely in no-limit. If they have the best hand to go, no matter how they play it there may be two or three or even more players drawing against it, also unlikely in no-limit. And their skill in setting up a bluff is minimized in limit for the quite obvious reason that successful bluffing in limit is far tougher than in no-limit.

Most of the time the bad limit players simply use the no-limit routine as an excuse to salve their pride. I recall a financially solid player who invariably snarled about the unfairness of a limit every time he got a hand outdrawn. He always bought far more chips than he actually needed, because he liked to have several big stacks in front of him. I used to tell myself that he had no business in a limit game until I finally ran across him in a no-limit game. Gone were the big stacks of chips and in their place a modest little pile. As far as he was concerned the game was still limit poker.

77

Sixteen Tons

Nearly all taxi drivers give you a lot of conversation, more even than barbers, because moving along there are all kinds of chances for some topic of mutual interest to pop up.

The weather is always a reliable standby. The last cabbie who trapped me opened with the heat, and in two minutes was telling me that he had promised his wife an airconditioner if she would stop being a dope. I only grunted, but it encouraged him to tell me that she was a mark for bargains and kept him broke, although they had no kids and he was holding down two jobs. I asked him how he happened to marry a dame who was so careless with money, and he said he knew her only about an hour when he proposed and was accepted. She had hailed his cab just after losing her job, he promptly got nose trouble because she looked sad, and they wound up before a justice of the peace. He even got stuck for the cab fare. This had happened ten years previously, but it had not cured him of the habit of talking instead of listening.

Not too many guys were as amazed as I expected when I repeated the story of the cab driver who ripped the romantic sound barrier to shreds. Far wiser than I, they simply regarded it as a variation of the marriage-trap routine, with the sucker taking the bait in minutes instead of the customary months or years.

The biggest reaction I got was from the two-job deal. Most of the citizens of my acquaintance are far more concerned with the disposition of their leisure time than with such inconsequential matters as ambition or expanding their cultural horizons. They usually give sober thought and consideration only to social activities, recreation, and hobbies, and consequently they could not figure that anybody would be so dumb as to disregard the more important things of life by taking upon himself the burden of two daily rounds of work.

The fact is that nearly everybody follows trends. For example, an author, probably lacking in talent, jams crude and raw sex material into his books and plays, knowing that the public goes for such stuff and that the critics probably will give it their blessing by calling it bold and lusty drama, because they, too, do not want to get out of step. Even a trend to go hatless gets enthusiastic support. Certain bald-headed men, usually tightwads, who should be delighted to appear less ugly by wearing a hat, give this a big play, even though their naked scalp scorches in summer and freezes in cold weather.

The general trend to take life easy as possible is so strong that anybody who gives most of his time to scientific or other pursuits, for the benefit of mankind or his own exaltation, earns a special distinction. He is spoken of as being dedicated, which is merely a polite way of saying that he is square. I had a secretary once who was just about as average as you make them. Her life was wrapped around three objectives, as far as the office was concerned: gossip, time off, and raises.

Poker players are not too different, yet sometimes you may collide squarely with a stalwart spirit in whom the flame of ambition has not entirely been extinguished. I recall a City Hall pressroom game a few years back that was still going near dawn. The big winner remarked—not without bitterness—that it was rather frustrating to stay up all night to acquire property, knowing that most of it had to be sloughed off in taxes.

78
Everything to Gain

At the high school I attended, the professor of ancient history made a habit of getting us in the mood for the doings of the Assyrians or Babylonians by posing knotty little modern problems before we commenced class work. He once asked us what attribute we must possess if we ever hoped to become a man in the true sense of the word. After kicking it around none of us came up with the right answer, which was "self-control."

The professor's lesson has stuck with me ever since, but the hitch is that I almost never think of putting on the brakes until it is too late. By that time I have done or said something that has busted up a beautiful friendship, or I have created a situation that I would give almost anything to change but cannot.

You can get all the advice you want, printed or spoken, about why you should not lose your temper or otherwise let go of your self-control, but the trouble is that usually nobody is around to shove it under your nose at the moment that you are triggering your emotions into action. If they paid a dividend for every time you told yourself that, if you had it to do over again, you would not, but would remain composed, practically all of us would be rich—unless they took it back the next time we slipped.

Poker players who lose control are automatically in trouble. If you are mad because you keep getting big hands trimmed, you might start fighting the cards by trying to make your bets win instead of your hands. Sometimes this works out, but nearly always you only sink deeper, because when luck is bad it figures to stay that way until in the natural course of events it changes.

About the worst thing you can do is try to rack up a player you are burning at, especially if you are sore because he keeps beating you. It almost always happens that no matter what you do or how hard you try he will wiggle out of the trap and you will be poorer and madder than ever. If you are burning at a player simply because he is a heel or otherwise obnoxious and gun for him in the game, it almost always follows that you will wind up second. This is largely due to the fact that, whether you admit it or not, your emotions are lousing up your judgment.

Those who are wised up on such matters will tell you that it will be awhile before the processes of civilization refine out of us such inconvenient and costly savage instincts as bad temper. If you are afraid that you will not be around when it happens, the best thing you can do is take the advice poker players give each other quite frequently: "Don't lose your head, it's the best part of your body."

79
Steve Brodie Found a Way

During the Reign of Terror in France when they were lopping off the heads of royal and noble characters at a pretty good daily clip, being a common citizen was comforting—usually safe. You probably would have laid any kind of price that inherited titles would never come back in style, and would have figured you were stealing something if you got action on this proposition, yet in about ten years it was the same as before, only worse. They jumped from what had been a kingdom to an empire, with an emperor and empress and a court swarming with princes and princesses, and assorted dukes, counts, and barons.

If you think things are so very different today you just do not keep up with the headlines and television newscasts. Plenty of people go nuts about almost anything connected with royalty. If they happen to live in a country that has to get along without kings and queens and descendants of feudal lords, they are always eagerly watching for the latest bulletins on the doings of families in the top money and social prestige brackets—especially if they include standout good-lookers whose hobby is collecting husbands.

The reverence some of us have for inherited position and wealth probably goes back to the time when a thousands-of-generations-removed ancestor got his kicks watching the doings of and getting the latest dirt on the tribal big shots. The compulsion behind this sort of thing, professionals in the psychology business may tell you, is the subconscious desire to be important. Since most of us cannot, we have to be satisfied with a remote-control arrangement. If this or something like it is not the reason, figure it out for yourself.

Anyway, there is no denying that celebrities of all kinds get a big play from most of us. What is the special charm about a king or a movie star or a sports hero or a famous general? They are different, they have something the rest of us do not have. If a Bluebeard who did in twenty or so beautiful wives somehow beat each and every rap and was turned loose, his agent could take his pick of juicy contracts, because he would have a celebrity on his hands.

Poker games have been known to take on a somewhat different aspect when a person of distinction is among the players. He may not be too celebrated as far as the general public is concerned (for example, he may be the best one-pocket pool player in the business), but he has something that sets him apart, which is good enough.

166

A distant relative of mine of the same name got himself elected a little while back to an important municipal office. From that time on my own identity in poker games became subordinate to the fact that I was kin to a big shot.

I was playing in a public-club game once and became aware that marked deference was paid to a newcomer who seemed to act as if the consideration was no more than his just due. I could not figure out the angle, because there was nothing about him that in any way suggested the reason for his claim to fame. The mystery was solved when a House man tipped me off to the identity of the distinguished visitor. He was the brother of a honky-tonk operator who had gone to the chair a couple of months previously for the rather lurid strangling of his lady friend.

80
"Potting" and Bluffing

Some years back, a hustler of my acquaintance made it a point to commence playing at his favorite public poker club around 6 A.M., or even earlier. His purpose was to get into a limit stud game in which nearly all the players were shills. The club operated around the clock, but usually in the early morning hours the stud game in progress had to be kept going synthetically until enough "live" players came in to put it on a normal basis.

Now offhand it might seem that the hustler referred to was taking all the worst of it playing with shills, House men playing their conservative best. However, it was precisely for this reason that the canny hustler wanted their business. He knew that he could "pot" them mercilessly, resulting in a profitable edge in chips when the game improved, or perhaps even sufficient profit to call it a day. The hustler's method? He would simply represent the best hand at every reasonable opportunity, well aware that the shill holding the top hand in sight would have to pass unless his hole card made his hand a cinch; and the hustler would almost invariably represent his hand as being best if *he* had the top hand in sight. He did not always make a profit, because now and then he would collide with a strong hand and take a loss if he did not outdraw, but he made enough to justify his daily habit.

This now brings us to the difference between potting and bluffing. Realistically, there is no difference, because in both instances an inferior hand is driving out a better hand; but, in volume of chip value, the difference is great. The hustler who liked to play with shills represented strength to win the antes and the initial bet by the player forced high, or represented strength if high in sight—if the pot contained little more than the antes. Bluffing is recognized as such when the pot is of relatively substantial value, and the representation of strength is backed up by a large wager, if the game is table stakes, or a bet the size of the limit, if the game is limit. It may, of course, be accepted as an obvious fact that the big wager in the table-stakes games figures to function successfully as a bluff more often than the full limit bet in the limit games, but bluffing occurs in the limit games, too. Dependent upon the way the play has developed from the outset of the betting, a player in the limit game may so apparently have the best hand that his opponent or opponents will pass when he bets, when the cards are out.

There is a certain type of player, especially in the table-stakes game, who habitually pots (or attempts to pot) notoriously conservative or "tight" players. He will either raise their high card or, if they have called an initial modest bet, wager a chunk if they have not helped on the subsequent turn of the cards. The potter, in the long run, invariably gets the worst of it. He gets potted himself by the tightwad, occasionally, when the latter is in a very favorable position, and also now and then runs into a stone wall when the tightwad has represented weakness by checking a cinch.

168

81
Folly to Be Wise

Playing it smart and cool does not necessarily mean that the Cadillac you are riding in is your own. It could belong to the chump you laughed at for taking the chance you turned down.

Sometimes the more you know the less you get. It often happens that you apply cold logic to an opportunity that comes your way and pass it up because you figure out a thousand reasons why it is no good. Then some poor, ignorant sucker blunders in who is too stupid to understand all the disadvantages and handicaps, and he winds up with nothing but money.

Smart poker players have all the best of it, but the suckers do not always lose. They just bow their heads and keep plowing regardless of odds and, if they hit a lucky streak, can wreck a game in nothing flat.

Poker game suckers—especially speedballs—have an outstanding advantage over other players. They get plenty of action because they are easy to beat, which of course makes sense. So when these adventurous boobs, who play one ace as fast as you play two, hold big hands or frequently outdraw the best hand, they accumulate rapidly.

Sometimes these soft touches act as if they seem to think that it is illegal to give themselves any kind of a fair chance. They are in the game to play, not to stay. So when they get lucky they make you believe they are trying to throw their money away but the cards will not let them. They are liable to get you so dizzy that you will start wondering if the percentages are not all wrong and the twelve-to-one shots they make win with stunning regularity are not actually one-to-five.

If I seem to be saying that the best way to play poker is to make like a sucker, give it a big discount. I am only trying to make it clear that suckers have their innings, and while they are at bat you might just as well put your talent in the deep freeze, because when you are bucking luck the other guy can use any substitute for brains and still beat you.

I like the true story I heard of the intellectual giant who poured his meager life savings into oil stock and loused up all the forebodings of his friends and well-wishers by making a million. He later admitted, when accused of having had an inside tip that he kept to himself, that he bought the stock because it was printed in a rich shade of green—his favorite color.

82
The Home Front

It may not be a bad idea if you are invited to play poker at somebody's house to find out if it is going to be a poker game or poker party.

In case you have a full social life but the idea of playing poker appeals to you, you may want to duck if you happen to be allergic to feminine squeals and general pandemonium. You also may not have a strong enough constitution to be seated at a table that finally presents a strange mixture of scattered cards and chips, undevoured food, half-finished drinks, and assorted impedimenta.

170

There is one thing about a poker party you will get hip to in ten minutes or less. You can take all your poker knowledge, if you think you have any, and give it the old heave-ho. Nearly everybody stays in every pot or may throw his hand away at any stage of the proceedings for such important reasons as giving a better ear to some gossip or fetching something from the kitchen. If anybody acts in turn or makes any other right move, it is purely accidental.

I was dumb enough the first time I sat in on one of these nightmares to line up a fancy play. However, before I could get it going, an appealing female seated next to me showed me her hand, which consisted of five unrelated cards, and wanted to know if it would not be a smart idea to raise. So I figured, "What the hell?" and from that moment drew three cards to flushes, continued calling in stud when beaten in sight, made the one-eyed jacks and red queens wild when I dealt, and played spit-in-the-ocean and other slightly exaggerated forms of poker with the best of them.

Now and then you run across some pretty fair poker in penny ante games when you are playing poker and not using the game as an excuse for a social gathering. You might even collide occasionally with somebody who can give you fits. The fact that you are playing for pennies is unimportant. Some boobs believe that because Nick the Greek or Joe Neversmile or other high-stake players make wagers only in the thousands that they are automatically top players. This is nothing but a lot of nonsense. Equalize the finances, and the tough penny ante player who never changed anything bigger than a quarter when he took out a stack might wind up standing them on their heads.

Further on the subject of poker games at home, where, incidentally, a lot of the poker in this country is played, some weekly or semiweekly games have become institutions. Frequently two or three different generations of the same family have participated, younger men taking over the places vacated by the passing of their sires or grandsires. Not all such games are in the penny ante class. Some very lively action takes place on weekends or more often in many a cozy basement or den.

Nearly all poker games are planned, but some just happen. As far as I know nobody ever took a nose dive in popularity for suggesting a little game when you are confined to the fishing camp by squally weather, or deadlocked in the jury room, or almost any other kind of situation that brings a group of men together with time on their hands and a craving for action.

83
You Can Outsmart Yourself

I recall among my juvenile reading pleasures Jack London's *Star Rover*. The main character while in prison somehow developed the power of projecting himself in spirit into other entities and thus escaped boredom by leading a series of very eventful lives on the side. In one of these he was a dashing cavalier and so famous a swordsman that none dared face him. However, he carelessly offended a square of the period, who promptly issued a challenge. The Rover knew the duel would be a pushover, because his opponent was nothing but a green hand, so figured he would toy with him a while before adding him to his collection. It turned out that the guy was so completely unorthodox and awkward that he confused the Rover and gave the fatal thrust instead of receiving it—just another case of the odds-on favorite blowing the decision because of overconfidence.

Possibly the height of overconfidence is crossing on a green light without looking. You are legally in the right, but if you happen to get knocked off in the process the only people who get real comfort out of it are your heirs.

The worst shellackings you take in poker very often are from rank suckers. You can get so cocky playing against them that you wind up outsmarting yourself. One evening in a no-limit stud game a snuffy old pigeon from a nearby small town was putting on a party, and everybody was getting his load except me. He was so dumb he would call pairs in sight with only an over-card in the hole and one or more cards still to come. If he happened to have a good hand he would give it away. He did everything wrong for hours, but I could not get a crack at him. Finally I was backed up with kings and he was high with an ace. We both caught small cards, and I nursed him along until just before the last turn, when I made a pretty good raise. I wanted to test him and also wanted to get some of his chips in the pot, because I was afraid I would pair in sight and would not win anything. He just called the raise, which I found very gratifying, because I was now dead certain that I had him. Neither of us caught anything on the final turn. He was still high with the ace and promptly bet the bundle. I beat him to the center and he showed me two aces.

You can even get overconfident with the best hand in stud if there is one or more cards to come. It may not be completely wise to get all your chips in even though you have all the best of it at that stage, unless the game is no-limit and you can take insurance. When you take insurance you simply bet that your hand will stand up, sacrificing part of your potential profit to be certain that you not only will not lose—no matter what happens—but that you will make a little something besides. You can usually get three- or four-to-one if it is pair against pair, much better odds if your opponent is trying to outdraw three-of-a-kind with a higher pair, or is trying to make a straight or flush. If the game is limit and you do not want to risk too much, all you have to do is stop raising until you see what the next turn brings.

Some boneheads will figure that you are chicken if you ease up with the best hand before the cards are out, but who wants to risk the family jewels? Plenty suckers could get nominated to the Hall of Fame for knocking off big dukes.

173

84
Stout Fellow

I played poker for years with a sharp hustler who had nothing but guts, yet who very often stood for being pushed around. If a popularity contest had been conducted he probably would have finished absolutely last, because he had two irritating qualities. He always managed to avoid violence while never really losing face, and, much more important, he was a good enough player to maintain a winning average year in and year out.

One evening an ex-heavyweight boxer of the tank town circuit, turned muscleman, who had been chasing double bourbons with vodka, got into our stud game and immediately promised to break a few arms if he caught anybody cheating. The threat was idle, because nobody in the game was smart enough to cheat, and besides, everybody was watching everybody else too closely. The big heel started losing immediately, and finally got his case chips in a pot with the hustler when the latter was dealing. I could see by the cards showing in each hand that the ex-pug was a dead duck, but the hustler, to my astonishment, gave up before the last turn. He admitted to me later that he knew he had a cinch, but said he was more interested in keeping his arms intact than in winning the pot.

On many occasions the hustler let himself be ribbed and needled without mercy, even by helpless lushes who probably could not have stood without assistance, let alone get into action. He usually seemed to enjoy it, which is understandable, because it is good business to have other players have their tongues hanging out trying to beat you, but he sometimes stiffened if the situation threatened to get out of hand. One night he casually remarked to a tough-talking stranger who had plenty of size going for him, but who had stepped a little too far out of line, that the time had come for a showdown. He suggested, without the slightest change in his normal tone of voice, that they let themselves be locked in a pitch-dark room, each armed with a loaded pistol, the winner to knock on the door. The antagonism ended pretty abruptly. When I asked the guy afterward if he had meant it, he gave me a double-talk answer to the effect that there is a time to pass and a time to bluff, the trick being to figure out which.

An obnoxious young punk, who could only have evolved from a spoiled brat, gave everybody a bad time every time he played, but the hustler was his number-one pigeon. I kept waiting for the slaughter, but the hustler was too smart to risk getting barred for clobbering a good producer, so he rigged up a deal to muzzle him the easy way. He bribed the porter, who probably would not have weighed a hundred pounds wearing two vicuña coats, to spill a drink in the punk's lap, knowing that it would produce a blast likely to be heard in the next county. When, instead of cringing, the porter set himself to throw a right cross, the victim lost no time going into the accidents-will-happen routine.

I had a deep affection for the hustler for two reasons. When he was in the game the monkeys who like to ride people gave me less attention—and if the cards broke even he was my meat.

85
The Intelligentsia

If you enjoy a swift kick in the teeth, try being nice to a sucker in a poker game.

The tough philosophy of never giving a sucker an even break is more than just a good rule, it is a necessary self-defense technique that keeps you from getting stomped. By all means be wary of that first symptom—pity. You beat a sucker so much you begin to feel sorry for him and drop your guard (for example, you give him action with a hand below your standard; or worse, because it is mere sentimental weakness, you show down a winning hand instead of betting). If you go real soft you get friendly and give him a pointer or two, overlooking the fact that you may be putting a club into his hands to brain you with later on.

I have yielded at various times to the human failings catalogued above and reaped nothing but dented dentures. One snuffy old bum who used a hearing aid and tottered when he walked, even though supported by a stout cane, whined a lot because he claimed that I always beat him, so I let him slip off the hook two or three times. He showed his appreciation later by checking an international lock into me when the cards were out. I can still hear his odious cackle as he racked me up. Another sucker to whom I had shown similar consideration put me in the middle against a pal of his who had top hand, and drained me of a stack of chips before he stopped raising.

When a sucker gets the upper hand he will often change from a pigeon to a hawk. He is not satisfied just to beat you; he wants to humiliate you, make you look bad, convert his victories into triumphs. These brief periods of glory and self-satisfaction are among the sparse rewards he gets out of the game, not counting the total fascination of the game itself. They serve to confirm his inner opinion of himself as a player, so he buys the idea that although he almost always loses, it is due to stinking luck and not lack of ability.

It may sound strange, but you are frequently obliged to play harder against a sucker than a good player. To begin with, a sucker's hand is much more difficult to figure. He also does not discourage easily, so you are rarely sure of a quick victory. If you make a strong representation at the beginning of a pot and pair in sight or otherwise strengthen your hand along the way, a good player often will quit, but a sucker will keep going as long as he can beat what he can see. So if you are in there with him and want to win you have to have the goods. Few suckers will stand to be bluffed.

If you add it all up, players in the sucker category, among other deficiencies, confine their thinking to their own hand and do not logically relate its value to the prevailing situation. Thus, you do not have to trap them, because they do this very efficiently themselves. They very likely belong in the company of those individuals, seemingly increasing in number, who have a limit of understanding, and beyond this is a vacuum in which ideas or nothing else can flourish. I once knew a crabbed old goat who had a similar theory about certain types of women, especially outstanding good-lookers. He said that after considerable study and observation he had come to the conclusion that quite a large number were retarded in their mental processes by having a blank space inside their head. He said this space acted as a buffer to the assimilation of large or complicated thoughts, although little ones could navigate the void.

The big reason that the penitentiaries are bulging at the seams is not so much the cleverness of the police as the stupidity of the

177

criminals. In the first place you have to accept stupidity as a premise in dealing with the criminal character, because only a nitwit would risk his liberty for the uncertain gains of crime. If you need further proof, no matter how smart they are in pulling a job, most criminals put a red flag on themselves afterward, such as tossing around double-sawbuck tips in night clubs.

86
Look Alive

In the days before a squat but popular four-cylinder automobile became a luxury item you did not have to be a keen student of human nature to figure out that the owner probably was ultra-conservative. If you observed that he wore a derby and placidly smoked a pipe as he chug-chugged along you could lay a pretty good price that he was nothing but a square.

The old saws say looks are deceiving and a book cannot be judged by its cover, but where people are concerned the opposite is often true. If you examine them closely you will find that in an astonishing number of cases the people you encounter every day are exactly what they seem, for the simple reason that the way they think somehow works through to the surface and is reflected in their physical and facial characteristics.

I used to make mental bets with myself about certain individuals I would tab this way or that based only on appearances. It is too bad that I was not doing business with a bookie because I had all winners. I finally gave up the hobby because it was not sporting

178

enough after correctly tabbing as a hellion a sour-looking frump who frequently breakfasted at my favorite cafeteria. She looked so much like the victim of wholesale frustrations that I figured she might be an exception to the rule. One morning, however, I was behind her in the cafeteria line and, because I was in a hurry and she was blocking traffic trying to make up her mind whether she wanted prunes or apricots, I timidly requested permission to move my tray ahead of hers. To be original, that did it. She screeched at the top of her voice that a drunk was molesting her and she swung at me with her umbrella, and only the fact that I was known in the establishment kept me from going to jail.

If you play poker with a total stranger for as long as thirty minutes, you can often get sufficient opportunity to confirm your initial opinion of him, which was based solely on appearances. You may not have deduced, as Sherlock Holmes may have done, that he is a bank teller or a paperhanger by some telltale sign unnoticed by the untrained eye, but you could have tabbed him as a heel or a right guy, a gent or a bum. Unless the stranger under your microscope is deliberately attempting to misrepresent himself (a most unlikely possibility) you can, more often than not, score a direct hit.

There are times when you are tempted to switch your opinion of a player, unless it is already good, in the light of some current happening—for example, after you have fattened your stack off him. A thing like this can cause you to soften, especially if you begin to think that your judgment was too severe and maybe he has not got such a conniving puss after all. However, the next time he outdraws you there is an immediate reversion to the original appraisal.

Let's face it. A pompous civic leader who looks like a stuffed shirt usually is. You cannot always be right, but when you have been taken for a ride by appearances it could be because the subject of your error was seen by you for the first time under exceptional conditions, for example in the tough stages of a king-size hangover.

87
Discipline or Disruption

In a barroom game one evening a player who had been refused credit by the House went berserk. Not satisfied with noisy obscenities, which nobody paid very much attention to, he tried to ignite the poker-table covering with a cigarette lighter. He managed to scorch it a bit, but the heavy canvas-like material did not catch fire. However, the House by this time had reached the limit of patience, and he was removed from the premises with less ceremony than one ordinarily follows in stepping on a roach.

A somewhat different situation occurred in a second-class public-club poker game. The bad actor in this case did not want credit, but was proving extremely annoying to the floor man, dealer, and other House personnel by demanding changes of cards with unreasoning frequency, cursing the porter, who was doing his best to satisfy the malcontent's wishes, and generally making a nuisance of himself. When he finally departed one of the dealers asked the floor man, who was acting manager, why he allowed the bum so much rope. "Why?" the floor man repeated, slowly removing from his mouth the cigar on which he had been puffing placidly. "Why? I'll tell you. If he comes in here tomorrow and uses the middle of the floor for a toilet, there's only one thing we can do: clean it up. He's the biggest producer we have, and the boss says he can do no wrong!"

There are, naturally, two widely separate points of view on the issue. In the average public game, barroom, or club, disorderly conduct, especially if continued after warning, is promptly handled by ejection, which, on occasion, is a bit less than gentle. Good producer or no, the House realizes that permissiveness on the one hand may cost the loss of player patronage on the other, even if the shenanigans do not actually involve the players themselves. The fact is, it goes even further than that, since witnesses to House subservience of such a nature naturally talk about it, assuredly no boost to the joint.

It has often occurred to me that, sooner or later, the 98 or 99 percent of the people of the United States, who have endured the hippies and white and black militants, are going to react, finally, as poker players do when one of their number persists in going too far. I have seen it happen many, many times. A bully or a pest or a drunk or a dumb extrovert or another undesirable will continue to louse up the game, resulting in annoying delays and exasperating all the players, not even excepting big winners. The degree of tolerance may be influenced to some extent if the offender is a loose sucker throwing his money away, but, eventually, some player fed up to the neck and maybe beyond will quietly say, "Look, Mister, we've had enough of that————!" And when these words are spoken, in the manner described, there is no possibility of misunderstanding. Even a drunk gets the message, and if he is half-smart, it does not have to be repeated.

88
These Things Happen

I have made reference elsewhere in this work to the "subtle needle." In other writings I have stated that cheating in poker games is rarely tried or accomplished. I now believe it is appropriate to present a potentially repetitious situation I once witnessed that could be classified as "subtle cheating."

The game was no-limit stud. The pot was worth about three hundred dollars when the cards were out. The player whose hand was king high in sight (no possible straight or flush), and therefore whose turn it was to bet, shoved his entire stack of chips into the pot. His opponent, whose hand was ten high in sight (no possible straight or flush), promptly called, making the total value of the pot nearly eight hundred dollars. The bettor, turning over an ace in the hole, said despondently, "A pair's good." The other player, whose cards were all red, a mixture of diamonds and hearts, flashed his hole card quickly, announcing, "Two eights," one of his cards in sight also being an eight. Then, without the slightest hesitation, he threw the five cards that comprised his hand into the discard, and raked in the pot.

I probably was the only player at the table other than the winner who was aware that the hole card was not an eight but a six. As every stud player knows, an eight and a six in the hole are easily mistaken for each other at rapid glance, and this is what the winner undoubtedly counted on when he hurriedly exposed his hole card and just as hurriedly got rid of the hand.

Now, explanations are of course in order, the first being that the winner did not proceed accidentally. He knew his hole card all right because he had looked at it more than once. Until the last card fell he was in position to win the pot legitimately or by bluffing if he paired in sight or drew an ace, and he also felt pretty certain that he could win if he paired his hole card (a six, as stated), because his opponent's first card was a five. At worst, he would have a good chance of winning the pot in the manner described, which he did.

The question arises, quite naturally, suppose his hole card had been correctly identified, what then? He would have been allowed to take back his entire last bet because he was beaten in sight by the king high and therefore, according to the rules of poker, could not lose his money by calling. So then, in effect, he was actually risking somewhat less than half of the pot value before the final bet and call were made. It also may be asked why I did not protest. The winner's hand was so quickly in the discard that proof of what certainly seemed to be a most successful cheating *coup* would have been impossible to obtain.

Nearly all expert no-limit poker players have certain plays that they favor, but I have yet to observe any that I would be interested in adopting. One such player, for example, likes to stand pat in draw when his hand is no better than two pairs or less. He sometimes wins pots with this play, because going up against a pat hand without one or even with a small straight seems foolhardy. He loses when he is not believed, and I think that a mathematical computation of the whole would reveal a net loss for this particular operation.

Another player likes to raise when his hole card is the same as the card that is forced high, or is being represented by his opponent. He, too, wins pots with this play, but again I am certain that the total investment in such instances would result in a net loss.

I have a few favorite plays of my own, but these, the reverse of the above examples, are based on representing weakness when strength exists. Occasionally, very rarely in fact, I will take a modest flyer the other way, but instantly crawl back into my shell if the angle I am shooting goes sour.

183

89
Keep Telling Them

The successful poker player has to put out for advertising the same as if he were peddling beer or cosmetics.

Since it cannot be done with television commercials or double-page magazine spreads, you have to resort to other methods, such as making like you are giving something away, or by putting on a convincing dumb act now and then. It costs but it is money well spent, because it adds up to pretty consistent action when you have the best hand. If the pigeons think they have a chance to beat you, they will keep trying.

Sometimes a legitimate fast play, such as raising from a deuce in limit stud when you are backed up, looks so hazardous from the viewpoint of most players that you get advertising value out of it. In spots like this, if you think the play has made an impression, it is smart to do a little vocalizing to emphasize your liberality, in other words the old talk-loose-and-play-tough routine.

When you have the disagreeable habit of beating a game pretty regularly, you attract a certain amount of unsolicited attention. As long as this shapes up to desire on the part of other players to knock you off, it is good publicity, but it works the other way if they get the idea too strongly that they will get their ears pinned back if they are in there with you. This type of situation requires that you take the rubber off the advertising bankroll. You have to play the small, legitimate hands a bit faster and show a bluff every now and then if you want to restore your opponents' confidence in your shortcomings.

Unexpected opportunities to advertise occur from time to time. You might be playing what you feel pretty confidently is the best hand, but as it turns out you win the pot only because you helped and your opponent did not. It is your cue at this point to make it plain that you knew all along that you were in there with the worst trying to draw out. This same crude dissimulation can be worked if you have the best hand in stud but are outdrawn in sight—by telling your opponent he had the best hand all the time.

A profitable form of advertising is to make a good impression on fast suckers. If you take advantage of every opportunity to knock out other players so you can take speedballs on head-to-head, they will figure that you are in their class and not only will be eager for your business, but will tell the other players how loose you are.

Another form of advertising is to make observations completely out of line with your true opinions—provided that you are not prejudiced against a little plain and fancy lying. You may have thrown away a better hand than a pigeon lost a chunk with, but when the pot is over you soften his disappointment by telling him you would have done the same thing he did. You also have continuing opportunities to make remarks on hand values or how you would play certain hands, and naturally should strain yourself to get across nothing but grade-A misinformation.

Pigeons like to feel that they are not the only ones getting clobbered. So if you have not got a legitimate tale of woe to tell them at pretty regular intervals, make up one.

90
Pesky Pedagogues

It is not too unusual for the sobriquet *Professor* to be tossed about in poker games. In some cases the recipient of the appellation may actually be an active or former faculty member of a school or a college, or may have been identified with some other form of instructional work. Nearly always, though, the sobriquet is used derisively, to mock the efforts of one player to instruct another, or to belittle a wiseacre's analysis of a recently completed pot.

There are several vexing reactions that may occur after a big pot is lost, among the most objectionable being the needling observations of the winner (if this happens) or—perhaps even worse—verbal chastisement by the game's "Professor" for mistakes that may have cost the loser the victory. In respect to the latter, the critic may be far off base if actually in possession of all the facts and circumstances, but, often not being in such position, is flagrantly illogical. As an illustration, the loser may have set up the play based on what he logically assumed another player in the pot would do, which did not occur, thereby upsetting his carefully laid plan, and making it seem that he had acted indiscreetly.

The above preamble is to set the stage for presentation (and dissection) of the issue of poker instruction. Just about all of the so-called experts (I am alluding specifically to those who write books that purport to "teach") seem to believe that an accomplished poker player may be created by didactics. I used the word *seem* purposely, because I am by no means convinced that these learned pedagogues sincerely believe that the formulae they offer for success in dull, involved, page after page of their trumpery books actually could be of benefit to anybody. Their advantage is that hardly anybody knows enough to challenge them, and the ones who could put them to rout naturally do not read their absurd books, or, if in some way exposed to their contents, react with amusement or contempt, or a combination thereof.

The fault, however, is by no means confined to the poker-text-book writers, as I pointedly implied by my references to the Professors of poker games who verbally project their erudite admonitions, criticisms, and counsel. In a rather definite sense they are even more obnoxious, because earplugs ordinarily are not available in poker games, so the Professor has a captive audience. The plight of an inept player, particularly a novice, is far worse, because he may be obliged, through politeness or policy, to listen in private to the dos and don'ts of his advisor, and figures to come out of such session baffled and confused—if he does not have the good sense to wipe it all out of his consciousness immediately.

I have in other works touched upon the business of teaching successful poker play, which I regard as just about impossible. Some basic instruction can be taught: sufficient capital; unremitting attention and concentration; high standard for initial pot participation; understanding of the other players, not only as to their normal ability rating, but also as to their standing in the game from pot to pot, and the possible effect some unpleasant or disturbing incident may have had on them; adherence, generally, to a method or pattern of play that has, after careful experimentation, proved satisfactory. Beyond these broad precepts I say, most emphatically, that a poker player cannot be taught, but must learn for himself.

All poker players, the most experienced and expert by no means excepted, make mistakes. Success is the reward of those who, in the long run, make the fewest.

91
Tempest and Sunshine

When you are in a bad streak playing poker, losing night after night and getting big hands that figure to win knocked off right and left, hardly anybody comments on it or even notices it; but if you are going well, especially if you have booked a few big winners in a row, you are a live topic of conversation and envy and might even get mentioned in some of the gossip columns.

Poker players are notorious for boasting about their losses, which perhaps accounts for their slighting the losses of others. If somebody dropped a chunk the previous evening, he will dwell on the disaster as long as he can get listeners. If, on the other hand, he made a good score, he will rarely mention it. As a matter of fact he does not have to, because you probably already have gotten the news down the street.

Another outstanding peculiarity of most poker players is the suffering they endure if they lose back the chips they have won. They will not take it too hard, generally speaking, if luck is bad and they get off to a bad start and stay that way, but if they get off to a good start and then skid, a bear rooted out of hibernation can be more amiable.

Some players who could no sooner give up poker than they could breathing make a habit of swearing off regularly. With certain of these players it is a self-imposed psychological treatment, but it is also a useful face-saving device if the regenerate is suffering from the malady known as the "shorts."

188

Like Tom Sawyer, who denied spilling ink on his textbook for form's sake and stuck to it from principle, players of a certain type consistently squawk for the same reasons. If they get too many big hands trimmed they are getting cold-decked, and when they win pots the cut is too big. Usually scant attention is paid unless the complainant gets too obnoxious, in which case he is told to take his business elsewhere.

If you want to get reasonable attention from poker players it is always better to tackle them any place other than in the game, unless you are giving something away. Almost any other subject, as a rule, is doomed to a skinny span of interest. Even the death of a fellow player has a good chance of getting the well-isn't-that-too-bad-it's-your-bet routine.

It is common practice in many games to make a pot occasionally for the runner (the porter or other House employee who brings food and drinks to the players and is available for assorted other services). The runner picks up individual tips along the way, but the pot is a sort of bonus. The suggestion for the pot is almost always made by a winner, and just as invariably the losers either refuse to contribute or do so grudgingly although the amount involved is trifling, a chip of ante value.

The safest course with nearly all poker players is to sweet-talk them or stand clear of them altogether when they are losing, unless you want to risk having your head chewed off. If you covet an invitation to somebody's fishing camp, a hint in that direction probably will fall on fertile soil if the owner has just won a big pot, especially if you were one of the victims.

92
The Crusty Set

Some people are so unblushingly cheeky that you can only figure they are making a career of it.

I was renting a house one time at a fancy figure, but the owner refused to replace an ancient coil-type water heater, although he knew I frequently had to heat water on the stove to shave without icicles. He was nothing but an immature creep, gangling and bespectacled, but he took himself pretty seriously—a smug paterfamilias. He had to be stupid because it was economically unwise to antagonize a good paying tenant who complained about practically nothing. During the controversy over the heater he deepened the gutter on the side street where I usually parked, for some screwball reason of his own about better drainage, although I warned him when he started excavating that it was totally unnecessary and created a hazard. Not long after it was completed, my car slipped into it and was hopelessly jammed against the concrete lining. As the derrick-type wrecker that was costing me a sawbuck maneuvered into position, my landlord suddenly came galloping out of his house nearby with his two small boys so that they could enjoy the show.

Some years back I was doing publicity for a large corporation whose head man could not have operated a peanut stand on his own without goofing. He was lucky enough to have a pretty fair staff, but his ace in the hole was the fact that he alone had contact with the board, of which his father-in-law was chairman. This way he took only bows, palming off his bloomers on some innocent victim whose advice he probably had disregarded. Once he junked the expensive furniture in his private office and replaced it with even more elaborate pieces at strictly playboy prices—largely to impress his new blonde secretary but also because he had a friend in the business. The day after the stuff was delivered he issued a tough economy directive.

Some notoriously tight poker players unhesitatingly put the blast on other players also allergic to giving their money away, but they are properly indignant if fingered themselves. Other players, who get the urge to quit if they jump off on top, scream to high heaven if they lose and the big winner decides to take the profit. The same thing happens in other departments, such as checking cinches. There are players who will denounce this as a very wicked and unethical practice—unless they are doing the checking. Among the cheekiest players are those who expect all kinds of consideration from the House, such as going on tab or getting staked, and who when on the receiving end are amiable and cooperative. When enjoying prosperity, however, they turn snooty and demanding and would not dream of making the slightest concession to the House. They are the first to quit weak games, complain about the House take and the service, and in many other ways give the House men a rough time. Hardly any game is without at least one unselfish soul, who louses up things with dull conversation and horseplay when winning but who will yell bloody murder when hooked if somebody breathes too loud.

A club operator, who was nothing but one-way and who would have copped any Oscar for unmitigated cheek, lost my valued patronage after a series of incidents that plainly indicated that he was a first-class heel as far as the rights and privileges of his players were concerned. About a year later he commenced an olive branch operation, and eventually induced me to visit his new establishment. There were two games going, one filled and a vacant seat in the other. Since we were just making up, I figured that he would be on his best behavior, so I took his word for it that the game with the vacant seat was as good if not better than the other. I could not use my own judgment because I had lost contact with his personnel and regular players. It took me only a few minutes, however, to discover that, of the seven players in the game to which he steered me, four were shills, two were stake-horses, one was cowing with the House, and all were tough.

93
Potpourri

Nearly all of the regular players in the public-club and other open poker games know that the "needle" is when, after you show down your hand, your opponent tells you to take the pot but stops you as you are about to rake it in, laying down the winning hand. Painful? Of course! And crude. There is another kind of needle, the "subtle needle," that could have originated with the Inquisition, or perhaps was one of the first forms of ancient Chinese torture. It is when, in a stud pot, you tap out against your opponent, whose hand in sight is higher than yours but who has shown weakness, and he hesitates long enough to convince you that you have him nailed. You actually have to believe that, because all your chips are in the pot. Then . . . down comes the boom! He had a *cinch* all the time. If you are half smart you will not openly show resentment, but if you *do* feel that such a reaction is indicated, go the whole hog—but be sure you have a good edge in weight.

It often happens that when you are watching a pot being played you sometimes are amazed at what seem to be the mistakes of one or both of the participants. If you are not wondering how one of the players can get himself so heavily involved against what looks like the best hand, you are silently criticizing the other player for not maneuvering to get more out of his opponent than he is getting. And, I might add, quite often you, the observer, have a better line on the proceedings than the principals. Well, it is not too difficult to figure out. Not being personally involved, you are more objective, and you know the strengths and weaknesses of both the players, or at least think you do. You therefore assume that each should be well aware of the other's moves, and you shudder inwardly at what you consider to be important errors. There is, however, one significant point that you may be overlooking. Your conjectures and reactions are based on the behavior of the players when *you* are the opponent and may not be applicable at all in the current instance.

It is an axiom of professional boxing that a fighter who has seen better days, especially if he was never top quality, will try to conceal his deficiencies by clowning in the ring or in training. It is a futile attempt at sangfroid to simulate confidence or, when the going is rougher than usual, disdain. Of such a boxer the knowing ones say, "He's washed up!" The same thing often happens to poker players who have never been too good, and who, in spite of long experience, are overmatched. They behave the same way as washed up fighters, everlastingly essaying dull and boring jests and witticisms and in their wake, a succession of injudicious (and costly) bets and calls.

Outstanding professional criminals usually follow a method or pattern in the consummation of their felonies, sometimes making identification and eventual arrest comparatively easy. To law officers it is known as their m.o., or *modus operandi,* Latin for "mode of operating or working." This foible of human nature, the indiscreet pursuit of habitual practices that can result disastrously, is not confined to safecrackers and other law violators. It is in evidence in many areas, but probably is most prevalent in poker games. Nearly every player has an m.o., that is, a basic method or style, with identical or nearly identical reactions in certain repetitive or closely related situations. The observant expert, accordingly, often can profit by cataloguing and keeping current his file of such information.

The most difficult criticism to level involves any proposition that, at face value, precludes the rationale that could be the basis for debate or even discussion. In these times there is constant recurrence of such indigestible "issues." Some extremist or deluded group will, for example, make outrageous demands that can only be branded by the recipient as "unnegotiable." However, when the matter is aired in the news media the words *problem* or *dispute* or *controversy* will be soberly employed, carelessly implying that there actually are grounds for acquiescence or adjustment, the same as if the demand had been legitimate in the first place.

The foregoing was written to serve as a preface to a subject that is, in my opinion, also in the category of outrageous misrepresentation. I allude to any so-called poker expert advertising that if his book on how to play poker is read, a guaranteed income will be the reward. Now, I have read advertisements of this kind that do not qualify or quibble. The claim was made in one case that the author won twenty thousand or so a year playing poker, and he offered his income tax report to prove it. That he actually won this money I have no reason to doubt, yet anybody could say that he made a certain amount playing poker, or tiddledywinks, and report it as income, and I am fairly certain that the internal revenue people would not start an argument about it. But, getting back to the business of such a guarantee as an "income for life," this is, in my opinion, sheer nonsense. To begin with, to make the kind of money the self-styled expert said he made playing usually with the same players, you would have to have requisite capital, surely in the thousands. And, even more important, you would have to find people to play with who have thousands to lose. It is like the old saw about the instructions the tenderfoot got about how to skin a bear. He was finally told that, of course, he must first *kill* his bear.

The other impediments to the success formula prescribed by the author are indeed numerous. Even if you happily have the

194

capital and are fortunate enough to find well-heeled boobs to play with, you still actually must *beat* them, and this does not always happen, no matter how smart or experienced you may be. The very best that can be said is that, in the long run, the good player will fare better than the inept player. The element of luck in poker is such that the most expert players càn have losing streaks that will last for months.

It should be added, finally, that if the guarantor of a lifetime income from poker based on his instruction is recommending play in professional games, such as those found in Nevada, and Gardena and other sections of California, he is only romanticizing. These games are operated strictly for the benefit of the House and are tailored to the transient trade. The rake-off and ante make it almost impossible for even the toughest hustlers to survive, and they figure to be better players, unquestionably, than the author himself, or any that he can mold. The fact is, savvy hustlers give such games a wide berth.

94
Money Mystery

You do not have to read whodunits for mystery kicks. There are all kinds of things you see or hear about every day that can prove very baffling indeed. The simpler they are, the tougher it is to find the answers, such as what certain married couples could possibly have seen in each other, or how some 24-karat phony can keep finding new people to fall for the thin baloney he slices.

One of the everyday mysteries that really stands me on my head is how some people can handle big deals with short money. If your income, in spite of your best financial gymnastics, just about keeps you a jump or so ahead of the sheriff, you have to be stunned when somebody you know who makes much less—and has a couple of kids to boot—invites you to visit the suburban home he has just finished paying for. And this same character usually comes up before long with a summer place and a cabin cruiser, or other items that run into important currency, while you are still feeling pretty good if you have handled your last income tax installment on time.

This business of money management is among the tricks that add up to finishing in the black in poker games. As any good poker player will tell you, operating with a short bankroll puts you in the precarious position of trying to outguess the cards. You cannot play the hands you want to play as they come, and let normal percentages take care of matters, but you must wait for something extra good. Due to the ante and other assessments it costs money to wait, and you have no guarantee whatever that the super deluxe hand will win or, if it does, that the victory will be justifiably profitable.

I figure that I am a pretty fair manager playing poker, even though I have all the best of it, relatively speaking, by not being in the short-money class, but I cannot give myself any medals otherwise. If I ever have a big enough chunk to swing a big deal, like buying a diamond mine or a block of stock about a yard long, it will be the first time. All I can do is clam up and marvel inwardly when people I know, whose take from honest toil is notches below mine, casually mention their latest market investments. I keep a sharp watch on leakage where chips are concerned, but in other transactions I must be nothing but a pigeon. I have tried many times to dope out the answer, but all I have wound up with is a headache.

Other improvident characters with whom I have discussed this acknowledge that they are equally mystified. Ruling out returns from successful ventures in crime, or legacies that they have kept mum about, we can only conclude that certain people simply are hip to the secret of making one buck do the work of several. Nobody should argue against frugality, which of course is a virtue, but you can carry it a bit too far. Who wants to squeeze the grease out of a doughnut before you dunk it in your coffee so that you can economize on shortening?

95
It Takes All Kinds

Oddballs may be found anywhere, but in poker games they stand out.

Every established game has one or more well-heeled players who appear at irregular intervals—usually about five or six times a year—and put on a party for the boys. Nobody knows exactly what motivates these players, theories ranging from a desire to be important to finishing second in a domestic row. If they savvy the game at all it is a carefully guarded secret, and they act as if it is against the law to stay out of a pot. Everybody gets his load except hard-luck players caught with a pitchfork while it is raining soup.

In a related category, there is another group of players who are more regular in attendance but not so fat. When their chips are low and they know they are at the end of the line as far as getting more is concerned, most of them know how to put on the brakes. By that time they are not playing to win but to stay. However, when they have plenty of chips or can keep buying fresh stacks, it is tough to hold them down. These monkeys are not trying to impress anybody or forget their woes. They just like the thrill of fast action. About the only way they can wind up winner is for the game to end before they go broke. I have played frequently with several who have never finished in the black. There was one who was pretty well on top once and had to quit because he was called away on some kind of emergency. He returned a couple of hours later and went for the works. I imagine he did not want to spoil his perfect record.

Poker players are the toughest audience in the world, even for interesting subjects—women, for instance—but certain wooden-heads cannot be cured of trying to show off what they seem to think is important knowledge. They like to babble about current best sellers or hit plays or scandalous items about celebrities, or similar chitchat you hear at cocktail parties and other stimulating social gatherings. No matter how many times they fall flat on their face they will wade in swinging. You cannot blame them too much when you stop to figure that people like that usually pick up what they know the hard way—not for enjoyment but just to be able to talk about it.

Some guys short-changed in the brains department but who have weight and bulging biceps going for them figure they can strong-arm their way to victory. So the sensible thing to do is to win their chips with an apologetic air. In a way these musclemen are like the gunslingers of the old west. They do not last too long because there is always somebody trying to get a reputation by polishing them off.

Poker paranoiacs are always beating other games in which the stakes are higher and the action faster. This is nice because most of the time they get shellacked pretty good, and it is comforting to know that they have a way of recouping their losses at the expense of strangers.

96
Get Your Best Grip

"It's not whether you win or lose, but how you play the game," is the punch line of an inspiring poem by the late Grantland Rice.

The chances are that not too many of the football coaches Mr. Rice knew personally would buy that offhand, even if they had a ten-year contract.

Let's face it. Nothing really counts but the results. That is what they pay off on. No matter how many tough breaks your team got or how much bad racing luck your horse had, the record books show only the cold figures. It is the same thing if the candidate you wanted to see elected did not make it because they stole him blind. He was the people's choice all right, but the other guy got the job.

Nobody can argue successfully against the stimulating sentiment expressed by Mr. Rice. If you give your all and play on the up and up, whether you win or lose you will not need dark glasses the next time you have to look in a mirror. The only hitch is that too much losing can bring on complications. Paying customers and such people as alumni get pretty tired of supporting a team that shows only moral victories. So while keeping it clean is important, there may be times when you have to fight fire with a blowtorch—if you figure there is no other way because your opponents did not read the poem. Of course you can always chicken out by dropping into slower company or by withdrawing from competition altogether—except maybe in tiddledywinks.

199

Short of cheating—which is tough to do and potentially unhealthy—poker players are not too particular as to how they win as long as they win. Each player has his own method, from the rank sucker who depends entirely on luck to the leathery hustler who throws every known curve, and whatever new ones he can come up with. Pleasure players are by no means exempt. If pressed, most of them probably would admit that if they lose it is no pleasure.

Poker is a game in which winning is so definitely the objective that it provides bad soil for white-armored Galahads. There is no such thing as a moral victory, unless you can find something to cheer about in the fact that, although they chewed you up, they beat nothing but big hands—and nobody could say he bluffed you. If you do not pounce on every legal advantage that comes your way you are nothing but a chivalrous boob, because when you goof it is a pretty safe bet that there will be no second primary.

Success is given top rating by nearly all poker players. If the dumbest pigeon, who cannot even spell *poker,* chops up a hand but rakes in the chips in spite of it, they will tell you he played it right—he won.

97
Glue on the Seat

Television quiz programs (especially before some were found to be rigged) made it possible for fortunate citizens to win cash prizes of staggering amounts, as well as Cadillacs and other assorted loot. Actually, it was but a happy commentary on the generosity of the big businesses that sponsored the shows, because all they got out of it was the privilege of advertising their products to a few million viewers.

A generation ago the same principle of sales stimulation was employed, but the going was much rougher. If you wanted to get in on the swag in the Twenties you had to have stamina plus, such as sitting atop a flagpole for a couple of months or dancing days and nights on end in the hope of being the last to collapse in a dance marathon.

Endurance records have always fascinated people, which is among the reasons city editors print pictures of married couples who have stood each other for fifty or more years. For the same reason anybody who has lived to be a hundred is a cinch to make page one without a press agent.

If poker game statistics were compiled the chances are some amazing marathon records would be revealed. Who would believe, for example, that many public-club poker games have lasted weeks—even months—without interruption except for an occasional few minutes at decent intervals for janitorial services or for a change of the tablecloth? Probably hundreds of players rotated during such lengthy periods, but the games kept going.

Long sessions at poker and other card games are more or less routine. Very likely the best-known character who made a career out of marathon sittings was John Montagu Sandwich, the fourth earl of that name, who held several important positions in the British government in the mid-eighteenth century, including those of ambassador to Spain, secretary of state, first lord of the admiralty, and postmaster general. Upon his retirement from public life he did almost nothing but play whist and other popular card games of the times. He hated to stop playing even to eat, and came up with the bright idea of having his meals served to him in the form of meat between two pieces of bread. Others imitated him, and today when we ask for "ham on rye" we do not even have to add the word *sandwich*.

Some poker players go on sprees, like the periodic lushes. If they show up on Friday you know they are good for the weekend or longer.

201

A couple of draw players some years back made history at the famous old Crescent Billiard Hall in New Orleans, long since extinct. They played for seven consecutive days and nights before being carried out, stiff as ironingboards.

In most cases players you leave in the game and who are still there when you return the next night do not have endurance records in mind at all. They simply have the hook in them and are trying to get even.

98
They Take You Back

Unlike old soldiers who never die but simply fade away, old poker players keep showing up as long as they can somehow make it to the game.

While getting hump-backed waiting for cinches, they like to tell you stories about things that happened even before the Spanish-American War. I figure that they go back that far because it is easier on their memory. That way they do not have to put themselves to the strain, because not too many people are still around who might throw a block on some of their statements.

We were talking about cheaters in a game one evening, and an ancient character who claimed he had played poker on river steamboats in the late eighties said it was too tough to cheat these days, not only because people are smarter, but because radical changes in men's clothing styles have made it almost impossible. In the old days when high-top shoes and waistcoats were standard, he went on to say, you had a chance to hide a cold deck and bring it into play at the right moment. It seems that elaborate contraptions were necessary of which hidden wires and springs were the mainstays. These gadgets made it possible to expand a pouch inside the trousers at the waist or in the waistcoat under the armpit just long enough to swap the legit deck for the cooler.

He said that success depended upon clever manipulation achieved by constant practice, but the cheater usually required an assist from an accomplice. The trick was to create a diversion, such as knocking a stack of chips on the floor at the right moment or spilling a drink in somebody's lap. One cheater worked with a confederate who only sweated games. The sweater would sit on top of the backrest of a chair, with his feet on the seat, and when his partner was ready to switch decks would lose his balance and fall to the floor with a crash. Our informant said he never hurt himself because he was an ex-professional tumbler.

We were told the champion of hard-luck stories by another near-centenarian who long before most of us were born frequented plush gambling saloons when faro was in vogue. Faro is a banking game, and the old man had a peculiar arrangement with one House that permitted him to continue playing if he went broke. He would send a messenger to his hotel to get a new bankroll from his wife with the understanding that if the money (an amount stipulated in advance) was not forthcoming, the play would be nullified whether he was on top or hooked. Once when this happened he hit the luckiest streak of his career. From the moment the messenger departed he could do no wrong, in fact he just about had the House ready to holler "uncle" when the messenger returned with the bad news that the player's wife not only had said no in fourteen languages, but had threatened him with a vase for disturbing her afternoon beauty nap. She had the money all right, and was innocent of scruples about her husband's gambling habits, but she was sore at him because he had left their suite that morning without walking her pet poodle.

99
Ignorance Is Not Bliss

Laboratory equipment is noticeably missing in poker games, yet it is necessary to run tests with some frequency if you have the sordid ambition to be a reasonably consistent winner.

The more you guess in poker the less chance your play has of being rewarding. The reason probably is quite obvious. If you have only a vague notion of the strength of other hands, you are usually doubtful of the value of your own.

This business of testing generally is the basis for success in almost any activity, no matter how routine. If you are constructing a skyscraper you just do not use the steel and other materials delivered to your job because they look good; you have them tested by experts whose business it is to find out if the quality is there. It also follows that no surgeon will even remove the wart from your chin unless he knows in advance if you are likely to bleed to death or jump hysterically from the operating table at the first touch of the scalpel.

Many poker players do not do much testing because they prefer the sneaky method of concealing the strength of their hand on the theory that it is easier that way to fool their opponents. They also figure to make a bigger pot because there are more stayers if there has been no raise. So they grope their way blindly through the hand, completely uncertain of how they stand as the play progresses, unless in the exceptional position, finally, of knowing their hand is best no matter what the strength of the other hands may be.

Just as in football where, in the poetic language of the late Grantland Rice, the game is usually won or lost "in the muck and mire of the line," so are most stud poker pots won or lost before the first turn, when the hand consists only of the hole card and the initial up card. If you have what you consider is requisite strength and raise when it is your turn to act, you immediately clarify the atmosphere. If one or more players remain you have a pretty good idea of where you stand and play the rest of the hand accordingly. If you do not raise and several players draw a card, you are almost always in doubt, and from that point usually the best you can do is guess.

Testing a hand by raising at the earliest opportunity whether the game is stud or draw not only spares you the uncertainty of guessing, but it also reduces competition, thereby increasing your chances of winning. You lose little if anything by knocking players out, because the ones who do stay pay double or more since sometimes there are additional raises.

Pigeons who play a hand cute by sitting on it until it gets beaten somewhere along the line usually invest more chips on the hand at that stage than would have been necessary had they started off playing it properly, and when their chance of winning would have been much better.

100
Count Your Fingers

Almost everybody knows about shyster lawyers and how they operate, but few of us realize that the legal profession has no monopoly on characters who handle ethics like a juggler, or who otherwise make free and easy use of their wits.

Shysters as a class try to overcome their lack of more substantial attainments by plausibility and trickery. If you take them on trust or turn your back at the wrong time you may be a dead duck.

The poker game shyster follows a pattern that includes such petty tricks as throwing less than the correct amount of chips in the pot and then asking for change, and going south with a chip or two when he shoves a pot to the winner. He also unhesitatingly claims the extra chip if some other player forgot himself and put up two antes. Helping people find chips they drop is one of his specialties. I knew one who worked a clever routine if he spotted a stray chip, a "sleeper," on the floor. He would purposely spill a couple of his own chips so he could get the stray unobserved. If the House dealer is a fink and overcuts pots for his own account, the shyster will cash them for him—on a fifty-fifty basis.

The poker shyster frequently employs a sneaky trick to influence players whose turn it is to act before him. For example, if the shyster has a hand in stud that looks dangerous and he sees a player hesitating about coming into the pot for that reason, the shyster—if he wants the other player to stay—will make a show of getting ready to throw his hand away. Thus reassured, the pigeon calls, whereupon the shyster moves in with a raise. This gag is worked differently if the shyster simply wants another caller to boost the size of the pot. In this case he will call out of turn to encourage additional action. He also may raise out of turn (or at least make a feint in that direction) if he thinks some player ahead of him may raise. He tries this when he likes his hand but wants to draw cheap.

Another favorite shyster trick is to switch the first up card and hole card if the up card is a big card and the hole card is small. Pigeons usually do not pay attention, so if he connects with the switched hole card he has a big pair out of sight—potentially far more profitable than if the pair were showing.

A shyster figures that almost anything is worth a try. If caught bluffing he may miscall his hand, hoping that the other hand will be thrown away automatically, which would make him the winner on a technicality.

Shysters are by no means restricted to any particular group or class of players. You will also find them among the pleasure players. Now and then the dumbest pigeon will throw a curve or shoot an angle. It is just a matter of the larceny coming out.

101
Damon and Pythias

If a major-league pitcher served up an easy one so that a pal on the opposing team could get a hit, or if a football tackle stepped aside to let an enemy halfback through as a sentimental gesture, you would have a situation paralleling brother-in-law poker.

No matter how you look at it there is no place for the don't-hurt-me-and-I-won't-hurt-you players in any game of poker. Even if they confine their cream-puff tactics strictly to those occasions when they are head-to-head, it has a bad odor.

Two players who have a peaceful-coexistence deal going may affect the winning or losing of pots by other players, because the reluctance of the two pantywaists to play against each other often influences their decision to stay or pass when the action commences. If one sees that the other is in the pot, he may want to get out of his way, and thus the natural fall of the cards is disturbed. This also works the other way, because the player who got out of his friend's way may have won if he had stayed; or by staying his friend may have won.

You get plenty of propositions to establish what amounts to an alliance. The spoken word is rarely used. The player who wants to get on a friendly basis usually waits until he is seated next to you, and when he has a good hand nudges you with his knee to let you know. In return for this favor you are supposed to do the same thing for him.

Without even considering the moral or ethical aspects I automatically reject all offers of collusion. I almost always know what my opponents have anyway (when the serious action commences and each player has been tested), and there are times when I go through with a hand even though I am certain I will have to outdraw to win. I never make a commotion when propositioned. I either ignore the knee signal, letting the other player find out the hard way that I am not interested, or I tell him privately that I could not possibly take advantage of his generosity.

When you are wise to players doing the partnership act it is very much to your advantage, because often you will be tipped off to the strength of one hand or the other. If not sitting alongside each other it sometimes is necessary for partners to develop a system of signaling. If you are observant it will not take long, as a rule, to figure out the semaphore. Two colluders kept me puzzled for a long time once until I finally discovered the key to their code. They used the spoken word, but on a routine and completely unrevealing basis. One word meant an ace in the hole, two a king, and so on down to the ten.

If you ever happen to have a strong angle—such as wanting somebody in the game to do you a big favor—and you figure it is smart to let him wallop you now and then, or you show your good will in other ways, that is a horse of a different color; but if you pull your punches or otherwise swap courtesies just to be palsy-walsy or because you are playing scary poker, you are in the wrong game.

102
One-track Mind

Nearly everybody has had the dismal experience during school days of being tripped because of inattention. If your mind did not go blank, your thoughts wandered to something interesting under the strain of a dull lecture, and all of a sudden the prof threw a tough question at you on the subject of his most recent remarks. Naturally you were caught flat-footed and felt and looked foolish. Not paying attention in the classroom may only have resulted in your getting a goose egg for that day's recitation, but this deficiency in a poker game could be a serious matter.

If you have a broken heart or are otherwise freighted with woe, you are simply asking for it, because in spite of the fascination of the game you are almost certain to slip into a mild coma now and then, thus distracting yourself from the more important business of watching what is going on. The same is true if you are on fire inside for some reason or other. While you are plotting revenge against the heel who you figure is trying to roll you for your job, you may overlook your hand or make a bad play of some kind that costs you a juicy pot.

Very few poker games are free of pernicious influences that tend to divert your attention. Some moldy character who keeps up with the news may project a discussion on the latest local crime story or start a bum argument about some fine point of foreign policy. Then some more enlightened player may want to talk about the big bet he lost when a foul was allowed in the fourth heat at Belmont. If the atmosphere is free of this sort of static, there are a thousand and one other distractions that muscle their way in and, if you let them, keep you from concentrating.

Nearly all good players focus their attention sharply on the proceedings if they are in the pot. They will know everything worth knowing, including an almost unerring appraisal of each opponent's hand. This is all right as far as it goes but is not quite enough. You should pay just as much attention when you are out of the pot, because it keeps you tuned in on the game. In this way you may pick up some new information about a player that you can fashion into a cudgel to brain him with at some future time.

103
The Price Is Right

Among other things you get wised up on if you play a lot of poker in barrooms and other open games is retail huckstering, covering a wide variety of items.

210

There is only one drawback. You are constantly exposed to a buyer's market, so if you should ever try to make practical use of such knowledge you would probably do better as a pawnbroker than a shopkeeper.

Favorite articles offered for sale at cut rates in public-club and tavern games include fountain pens, cigarette lighters, and assorted jewelry. You also frequently have the opportunity of acquiring the miscellaneous prizes of iron claw machines, especially alarm clocks, wallets, and flashlights. There was one character whose sole occupation was making iron claws disgorge. He had some method known only to himself of dredging these reluctant machines of their treasures. He appeared almost nightly with a big bag of spoil. I once gave him a buck for what seemed to be a top quality alarm clock, but the thing ticked so loudly I could not sleep in the same room with it.

Other opportunities for bargains also come your way. Such commodities as watches, luggage, dresser sets, and golf clubs at extremely attractive prices are not uncommon. If you happen to know that the seller is a right guy and you will not have to handle anything you buy with asbestos gloves, you can sometimes do all right for yourself.

I knew a conniving little stinker (finally barred from every joint in town) who made a pretty penny with a con routine that he would vary from time to time. His favorite dodge was to button-hole some chump and offer contraband French perfume for a song. The sample bottle not only was the McCoy in appearance, but also had a faint bouquet of the genuine article on the outside of the stopper. He told me that his boldest stroke was to sell a dime's worth of prepared chalk for a sawbuck to a junkie who thought he was buying a bundle of fixes.

Some poker players who go broke hate to give up without a struggle. The game is good and the evening is young. After all, who needs a watch to find out the time?

I played a lot of poker with an industrious little chump who peddled dry goods to small stores in rural communities. He kept his stocks in the trailer he used when on the road. When the going

211

was rough he would simply go get enough socks, handkerchiefs, and underwear to finance another stack or two.

One night a player sold a new suit and a hat and a pair of shoes, and not long after went broke for keeps. There was nothing unusual in items of that kind being sold except that in this case the player was somewhat inconvenienced. He happened to be wearing them at the time and he had to sit around in a tablecloth until somebody went to his room and fetched his other clothes.

104
Epicures

I was shocked one night when one of the players in the poker game with me polished off a jumbo hamburger sandwich with all the trimmings, followed by three hard-boiled eggs, and then went out to a steak dinner. I was shocked because he usually made it a couple of sandwiches and five or six eggs before doing any serious eating. This particular evening his appetite did not seem to get going until around midnight, when his customary snack of three or four bags of buttered popcorn and salted peanuts was doubled. It was nice to observe that he was keeping up his strength.

Thoughtful people are always telling you that big eaters dig their grave with their teeth. The trouble with the people who say this is that they also usually eat much more than they should. They may not be quite in the same class with characters who indulge in such items as steak and potatoes or spaghetti and meatballs for breakfast, and who walk around with their big barrel belly like pregnant women, but they are doing a fair country job of overeating without even half-trying. The fact is that just about everybody overeats, if you relate food consumption to physical requirements. Your body would have to have a pretty good furnace to consume without unusual wear and tear all the extra fuel you put into it, as a rule.

Plenty of eating and drinking goes on in all poker games. If you are playing at somebody's house you have to hold out until the refreshment period, but in other games you eat and drink at will. If you do not happen to think of it yourself, somebody else gives you the idea. Some players seem to figure that it is a legitimate part of the entertainment, that they are supposed to stuff themselves if they want to have a good time, the same as at a picnic or wiener roast.

One of the things that always puzzles me is how certain players not only drink steadily, but work variety into it. They will switch from beer to coffee to soft drinks and even such items as orange or tomato juice and then back to beer or maybe highballs and keep up this routine for hours, meanwhile not neglecting solid food. Usually the ones who do this are nonsmokers, which is either a boost or knock where cigarettes and other forms of nicotine poisoning are concerned—dependent upon whose payroll you are on if you qualify as an expert in such matters.

The subject of eating and drinking in poker games reminds me that I learned, among other things, that there is more than one way to come up with a lost weekend. One Saturday afternoon a shy little stranger got a seat in the game and immediately started on a black-coffee kick. The more cups he tossed off the higher he got, which we found puzzling because coffee on its own has no charge. It turned out, however, that the demitasses were getting a pretty good assist from a small bottle of high-voltage brandy in his inside coat pocket. On another occasion a big fat slob who drank nothing but milk—but plenty of it—got roaring drunk before our mystified eyes. We learned later that he had arranged with the porter to bring him, as he ordered it, nothing but milk—provided that it was spiked with a double shot of vodka.

105
Checkmate

A couple of high-powered chess players with whom I was having lunch one day engaged in a mutual gratification contest for my benefit, to emphasize the fact that chess is the one and only game uninfluenced by luck. They dismissed bridge with a deprecatory gesture because a novice with good cards can trim an expert. Poker they gave the lowest rating of all and very likely would not even have included it if they had not counted on my picking up the tab.

Poker is a tough game in which to win an Oscar. You can get a reputation as a good player if you work hard at it, but who wants to cut his own throat? Besides if you find yourself in a sticky losing streak you might get to look so bad that even the pigeons will start feeling sorry for you. The only thing that counts in poker is results. If you do not win the pot you must have done something wrong.

There is a relationship between poker and professional athletic league play, because the team that comes out on top never wins all games. The best the champion can do is have a bigger number in the won column than in the lost column. It is by no means unusual in baseball for the club that has a stranglehold on the cellar to polish off the high-flying leader, sometimes even sweeping a series. However, the payoff is still on the highest percentage.

The very best that the very best poker player can do is have a high percentage. It just is not possible to win every time you play. If you can come up with a .750 average year in and year out you are plenty hot and will look better in your league than the best team the Yankees ever fielded.

The characters beating the drums for chess goofed in at least one important particular. In maintaining that in chess, as opposed to bridge, poker, and other games, the better player always wins, they overlooked the fact that the same is true of bridge and poker as far as the end result is concerned, even if along the way the element of luck makes itself felt. The poker and bridge experts win in spite of circumstances and conditions sometimes beyond their control, therefore overcoming hurdles and handicaps from which the chess experts are entirely free.

I probably could not become an expert chess player if I dedicated the rest of my life to practicing clever methods of capturing my opponent's king, because I am a natural bust at precision games, mental or mechanical. However, this does not prevent my having the opinion that luck has to creep in occasionally. If your opponent can tie you in knots there is always the possibility that he might be steamed up inside about something which will throw him off his game, and you will wind up beating him—by luck.

106
Freeloaders

The instinct to get something for nothing is so strong in most of us that it keeps a lot of people employed, such as the bunko squads of big city police departments, the peddlers of Irish

215

Sweepstakes tickets, and about half the residents of Nevada.

Getting something for nothing is mixed up to some extent in almost everything we do, and it is not always money that we are after. Perhaps many of us, in our righteousness, will indignantly deny this where we are personally concerned, but honest probing can prove revealing. Inherent urges are not always part of our conscious thinking.

If your income is not from salary, fee, commission, interest, pension, public assistance, or some other stable source, you are nothing but an adventurer living by your wits—even if some rich relative gives you a substantial handout from time to time. Accordingly, you are a professional in the business of getting something for nothing, and should not be confused with the honest souls who know where the rent money is coming from and are mere dilettantes at cards or other games of chance, or who do their speculating in the business or investment fields.

Poker probably is among the very few games of chance where getting something for nothing may be both a primary and secondary consideration. There is a procedure that may be followed in poker games that theoretically provides free smokes, food, drinks, tickets to sports events, and miscellaneous items. All you have to do is "pot" with one or more other players with the understanding that the first of you who wins a pot of a minimum amount is stuck for the bill.

Potting may be and frequently is a rather congenial arrangement between two or more players who make a sporting proposition of it. There is a type of player, however, who regards it with a cold business eye and picks nothing but liberal pigeons to pot with so that he can freeload on sandwiches and refreshments and also lay in a supply of cigarettes or whatever else they happen to be potting for. He can win pots too, and sometimes does, but the free-doings percentage is all in his favor.

Since potting partners are concerned only with the monetary value of the items, not the items themselves, some astute potters translate this into practical use and stock up on supermarket and drugstore staples. I knew one career potter who figured the weekend was a total loss if he did not wind up with a king-size bag of free groceries.

107
Life of the Party

Some people are so unspeakably dull that when misfortune traps you with them even your best efforts seem feeble. They usually are almost entirely unresponsive, so you have to keep changing the subject to maintain what at least has the appearance of a conversation.

An acquaintance of long standing would occasionally drop into my office, and for perhaps two minutes the scene would be reasonably animated, but after the "what's new" routine he would just sit and stare vacantly at me, responding with parsimonious brevity as I desperately tried to touch upon some topic that would jar him from his zombi state. As a rule I would give up in despair, announce that I had a near due appointment, and steer him to the elevator. When we reached the street I would inquire which way he was going, so that I could shake him off by heading in the opposite direction for a quick walk around the block.

There is always less restraint if at least one member of a small group, assembled for lunch or some other social purpose, is uninhibited and loquacious, or nearly so. His presence or even expected presence automatically sparks the others. If the conversation is in high gear anyway without his assistance, there is always the comforting assurance that reserves are available if needed.

217

Many a party or other social function is saved because one of the guests—perhaps thoughtfully invited for that very reason—has the ability to loosen up the others. It might be argued that if there is no paucity of stimulating beverages the loosening up will occur in the natural course of events, indubitably a logical conclusion, but if spearheaded by an amiable personality there is an advance guarantee that a good time will be had by one and all. Even a brash extrovert, too dumb to quit while he is ahead, can prove useful on occasion.

In poker games there is no need for a personality boy, but just one player of the right kind can make the difference between a lively, animated session and one that finds the players just going through the motions. Even the losers figure to get bored if there is nobody to drive the play. When there is, which guarantees plenty of action, even the tough players frequently yield to the temptation to lower their sights and get into the swim. After all, such antics as extra raises "just to build a pot" and betting in the "blind," hoping that the hole card will justify the optimism, can be mighty inspiring—provided you are lucky enough to be holding your share of winning dukes. If there are two or more "drivers" you can be pretty certain that the other players (with rare exception) will become infected, resulting in what is known to the fraternity as a "wild" game.

108
Vendetta

In Poe's "Cask of Amontillado," Montresor, an Italian nobleman, lures Fortunato, also a nobleman and to all appearances his best friend, to a remote corner of Montresor's wine cellar and family burial vaults—deep underground and far removed from the possibility of assistance. Montresor tricks Fortunato into letting himself be chained to the wall and then calmly seals him in, slowly placing stone upon stone while Fortunato vainly begs for mercy. It seems that Fortunato had been in the habit of pushing Montresor around but Montresor could not afford to show his resentment. He bided his time, and at last the chance for which he had planned so carefully arrived. While the carnival was in progress and nobody knew they were together, Montresor took his revenge in classic style, with impunity.

Montresor got away with his diabolical scheme, but wine cellars deep underground are not so plentiful these days. So we have to think of other measures to even accounts with certain of our dear friends who seem to take great delight in dealing us misery.

There frequently is some player in a poker game who keeps getting in your hair. It can be a negative situation. Maybe you just do not like him because you know he is a phony but nobody else does. Much worse, maybe you suspect he makes you for one.

Most of the time your blood pressure is on the rise for some more definite reason, such as some obnoxious bully who gets by on his muscle giving you a hard ride. I have had it even from strangers. The payoff once was that after keeping the spurs in me for hours the guy who was on my back realized he had me mixed up with somebody else.

I have worked up a few king-size resentments, but have it in most of all for any player who has the disagreeable habit of playing too lucky against me. When you tangle with such a player, if he has the best hand it stands up, but when it is otherwise he draws you out. This is something much more serious than mere words or attitudes, and inspires me with an unholy passion for reprisal.

Gunning for a certain player by no means figures to be a rewarding experience. You may sit for hours without a chance to work him over, and meanwhile if he is getting the breaks it is even worse for your blood pressure. The net result is that it figures to louse up your judgment, you get impatient or overanxious, and first thing you know the score is even more lopsided against you.

If you must take out after a poker player simply because you do not like him, borrow a page from Montresor, who sealed up his good friend Fortunato and threw the trowel away. No matter how much you may want to knock him off, seduce him first with kindness and a smile. It will be a lot easier to hang one on his chin if his guard is down.

109
What Have You Done
for Me Lately?

One of the surest ways to win friends and influence people in poker games (and plenty of other places) is to be a consistent loser. If otherwise, you would make a lousy candidate for public office should you happen to need the votes and support of your poker associates.

Some poker players are very much like politicians. They forget all about the many times they may have trimmed you, but the first time you knock them off they act as if you have always done it and they make a speech about how lucky you are. If you do forty-nine favors for a politician but for some reason cannot do the fiftieth, he forgets all about the forty-nine and will throw you to the wolves at the first opportunity.

Among other things I have learned about poker is the fact that you cannot judge a player's ability until you have seen him in bad luck, because almost anybody looks good when on top. The same goes for nearly all players as individuals. The gracious, agreeable player is subject to change without notice into a king-size sorehead. He will give you the "good buddy" routine until it runs out of your ears, as long as the going is smooth, but when he stops getting the breaks he is liable to insult you if you ask him for a match.

I read somewhere once that it is characteristic of card players of a certain nationality to snarl at winners. I do not necessarily disagree with this report, but as far as poker is concerned no particular nationality has the market cornered when it comes to abusing players who make winning an offensive habit. Some of this comes from chronic losers, and is just another way of moaning, but sometimes sneaky tough players are guilty—to divert attention from themselves.

It is pretty hard to dislodge the gripers who get on your back when they finally absorb the irritating truth that you are not only ahead on your play over a lengthy period, but figure to continue drawing dividends. If they are in pots with you and collide with the best hand, they will tell you that you are tight and play only cinches, and if you are in there with the worst and draw out, you still get a verbal shellacking for being a greaseball. When they beat you they omit flowers, so all too often you have only the poor consolation of adding to your stack of chips.

110
Color Scheme

While still a potential juvenile delinquent, I spent considerable time on the docks of New Orleans. Among the fascinations was watching the unloading of banana boats. As each carrier left the ship's hold with a bunch of bananas slung across his shoulder, he passed a checker who not only tallied the load, but told the carrier, by mentioning a flag by color, to which freight car he should convey his burden. The idea was to segregate the green, not so green, and almost-ripe fruit for long, medium, and short hauls.

Poker players also may be grouped as green, not so green, and mellow, but their classification is not quite as simple as the cargoes of the Central American banana boats. You may make a preliminary guess that sometimes stands up, but frequently find it advisable to go into reverse. One of the big reasons for this is the fact that plenty of players look good winning and terrible losing, so you have to give them a fair test under both conditions.

It ordinarily is not too tough to get hip to green hands even on short acquaintance. They tend to use corny terms in describing hands and situations and usually are bumblers when dealing or otherwise manually engaged. If strangers with whom you play are smoothies handling the cards and chips and their nomenclature is in keeping with the less colorful terms you and your vile companions are in the habit of using, you may safely put them at least temporarily in the not-so-green category. If subsequently they come up with some fancy plays that cause you to think that they may be doing postgraduate work, get your best grip.

Poker games do not provide form sheets, so when you start playing in a game where there is a stranger or two it is not too unusual to try a shortcut by getting whatever dope you can from one of the other players or a House man. Of course there is always the risk that somebody else's appraisal may be considerably off the mark—either as the result of poor judgment or because some wise guy deliberately gives you a bum steer.

111
Hemophiliacs

One thing all of us should be in the habit of doing is losing graciously, because we take it on the chin with great regularity. If it is not money or some object that has material or sentimental value that gets away from us, we are on the short end of something else, such as an election or romance or hoped-for break that fails to materialize. Competitive sports produce bumper crops of losers every day, because (barring ties and dead heats) only one team or one contestant or one horse can cop the duke.

With all this experience you would think that we would take losing in stride, with no more show of emotion than hysterics or homicidal manifestations. Yet many of us simply cannot accustom ourselves to shellackings, being deficient in the stuff of which philosophers are made. The fatalists who merely smile with a tinge of bitterness if the hot horse they bet on stumbled at the gate and finished far out of it are not too plentiful.

The cold truth is that few of us get through a whole day without squawking about something, if only the weather. If you play poker or other card games or dabble in other areas where chance as well as skill and experience is a factor, you are in a class that produces the most outstanding squawkers, because there is so very often something to squawk about. No matter how weighted in your favor the probable result may seem, it does not always work out that way, and your consequent displeasure has a good chance of manifesting itself in a vociferous bleat. The fact that this changes nothing is immaterial. You figured to win but you lost, so you squawk.

Squawking in poker is not always a vocal exercise. You can squawk eloquently by inoffensive little acts, such as throwing the cards on the floor or sailing them through the air or slamming them on the table. A classic gesture is to tear up the deck—appropriate retaliation for its perversity. Some squawkers just gnash their teeth, grip their chips tightly, and glare about like sinister television villains. Others find comfort in assorted odd ways, such as picking up their chair by the top of the backrest and grinding the legs into the floor. I have seen players, exasperated by a perfidious run of the cards, grab a handful of chips and hurl them into the farthest corner of the room, a form of squawking that the porters think should be encouraged because it lightens the dull chore of sweeping. A loser on the psycho side will occasionally chew the cards. I heard of a guy who ate a couple of aces that got trimmed for his case money, but I was never able to verify the story. They say he did it without condiments.

Many squawkers are good for laughs. They develop an unconscious style from the long habit of pouring forth their laments when the breaks go against them.

In games where there is a House dealer there is far more squawking than in those games where everybody deals. The reason is simply that squawkers have somebody to blame who gets paid for listening.

Some squawkers use the melancholy approach. They neither bleat nor throw the cards around but like sympathy, and, with slight or no encouragement at all, will tell you how many big hands they got cracked or the size of the pots they lost because somebody drew out on the last card.

Grumbling squawkers are just plain mad and remain that way until their luck changes.

Some guys squawk even when they are winning. They go into their act if they lose a pot or if the pots they rake in are not big enough. Everybody in the game pulls for winning squawkers—to catch the measles.

Most squawkers will tell you that they just have to let it come out, but occasionally you will find one who goes the silent martyr route. An old hustler told me of a player in the same game with him who could not win a pot for hours and yet kept quiet and even wore a wan smile. The hustler could not resist asking him how he could take so much bad luck without even a single moan. For a reply the player reached inside his shirt and came out with a handful of blood. "And you think I'm not suffering," he said reproachfully.

112
Serves Us Right

I once made history by finishing first in an argument with the service manager of a big automobile agency—but only because he made a slip. I had come in to have the brakes on my car adjusted and, when told that relining was needed, permitted myself a mild beef, because the brakes had been relined about two months previously. It was at this point that the service manager goofed. He denounced the material as being a poor grade of compressed paper suffering from dry rot. It seems that he momentarily overlooked the fact that his own shop had done the work.

People do not bore you today with instances of outrageously bad service, they buttonhole you if they have a story with a miracle twist—such as somebody giving them their money's worth. The way things are now you feel like bragging if you happen to get a good shoe shine.

Just offhand you would not associate service with poker games,

226

but it is a factor to consider. If you get bad service in a poker game it can cost you pots and also maybe get you a working over in case the rise in your temperature gives you some phony notions about your ability as a battler.

Most of the crummy service you get playing poker is from the House dealer or the House man running the game. Misdeals, players acting out of turn, incorrect amount of chips thrown in pots, mistakes in fixing side pots, and general lack of interest in the proceedings are among the major items of bad service that House men sometimes give. If everybody deals there is an understandable increase in the number of mechanical errors.

Some people like to tell you that poker game mistakes may equally be to your advantage or disadvantage and in the long run will break even, as is the case with good luck and bad. There may be something to this, but when the pot is over the only one who will buy the theory is the winner.

There is a silver lining to the bad service you get in poker games and elsewhere. It is a way for people who have been pushed around a lot in the past to say, "If you don't like it, lump it." In spite of recessions and depressions that will come and go, enough basic changes have been made in our social system to eliminate forever the servility that too often used to be a part of good service.

113
From Where I Sit

Among the many heroic actions history records, the one that stands out is the charge of the Light Brigade during the Crimean War. It may be argued that Tennyson's immortal stanzas turned the trick, but other dramatic and gallant deeds also have been immortalized in prose and poetry without quite capturing the imagination as did the mad, suicidal onslaught of the six hundred British light cavalrymen that fatal day at Balaklava.

As I see it the utter futility of the charge, brave as it was, earned it top billing over anything else before or since. As a matter of fact that charge was so splendidly foolhardy that it was considered nothing but a top-brass blunder. However, at least one romanticist has attempted to establish the theory that the order was forged by one of its officers so that the Light Brigade could get at an Indian potentate in the Russian artillery command. It was a revenge deal, because the potentate had ordered the massacre of the garrison and civilians of a British outpost in India some time previously.

The big reason, though, for the charge being considered an all-time high in military indiscretion, while at the same time an epic of valor, still remains the fact that a single brigade of light cavalry hurled itself against a powerful army. If the army had been on the march or in bivouac and the charge a hit-and-run maneuver, it not only would have been heroic, but even to a certain extent logical, and therefore probably would not have achieved undying acclaim. In their attack the Light Brigade not only had nothing in the way of surprise in their favor, but they knew they were colliding with a vastly superior force of infantry, cavalry, and artillery—in other words, a big, tough army in *position*.

Poker players are always saying that position is everything in life, but they usually are thinking of it in terms of the game. Actually, position in the game as a play develops is so important that very often it may mean the winning or losing of the pot. If you are in an advantageous position and can move other players out by raising, your chances of victory are improved at least 100 percent. If you are playing stud, your position in the game can prove costly if a reckless bet is made by a player on your right, whose hand you have topped, but who is driving you into players on your left who could have you topped.

Position in a poker game has other aspects of great importance.

If the game is in a tavern, for example, it is a pretty good idea to be seated against the wall so that you can see what goes on all about you. You may find that in such a position you have a better chance of ducking under the table in case a brawl breaks out elsewhere in the establishment, and such objects as empty beer bottles are whizzing through the air.

114
Huey Might Have Done It

The average poker player may forget such events as an anniversary or a birthday, but when it comes to recalling some big hand he lost with, he is practically a memory expert. If you are indiscreet enough to ask, you will get every detail of the play including who was in the pot, what each had, how many raises there were, and maybe even how the winner was dressed. The punch line usually has the last player on the final turn catching the case ace to "bust out" in sight with two, or some pigeon making a middle straight, or some equally sensational tough break that caused the victim to blow the decision.

There is something about losing a big pot that sticks when the best hand is nipped at the wire by a long shot. No matter how many times you may have come from far out of it yourself, your soul recoils at the recollection of almost certain victory torn from your grasp at the last moment.

You can hear all the stories you want about big dukes that went down the drain and usually it is the same old record. However, if they were giving blue ribbons for these unhappy occurrences, I would vote for the poor soul who could not win a pot in a fast draw game all evening, but who finally had everybody by the throat in the biggest pot of all. He had four kings pat with an ace but threw away the ace and drew one card as a deception maneuver. The discard had to be reshuffled for the last player, who had three aces to go, and he wound up with four.

The football coach whose team is up against it, especially if it is homecoming day, knows that he is in for a long afternoon. This is something like the way you feel playing stud when more players than you want are in a big pot drawing against you. Every card that falls could be the killer, and unless you are lucky enough to grab some help yourself, you cannot relax until the final turn is over and you know you are safe.

Stud players use a famous commercial slogan when the last card to fall knocks them out of a big pot. They will tell you that the hand was "good to the last drop."

The reason more pots are lost on the last card is the simple fact that there are more possibilities of all hands helping with four cards to draw to. Nevertheless it is hard for losers to take and has not done anything for the suicide rate.

I knew some disappointed poker players who bemoaned the untimely passing of Huey Long because they had hoped he would eventually get around to keeping a reported campaign pledge to outlaw the last card.